DATE DUE

DEMCO 38-296

THE CHANGING
BALANCE OF POWER

Riverside Community College
Library
4800 Magnolia Avenue
Riverside, CA 92506

D20 .H544 1999
History of the modern world

Marshall Cavendish Corporation
99 White Plains Road
Tarrytown, NY 10591-9001

© 2000 Marshall Cavendish Corporation
All rights reserved. No part of this book may be reproduced or utilized in any form or by
any means electronic or mechanical, including photocopying, recording, or by any information
storage and retrieval system, without prior written permission from the publisher and copyright holder.

Consultants
Professor Charles Ingrao, Purdue University
Professor Ronald J. Ross, University of Wisconsin–Milwaukee

Created by Brown Partworks Ltd
Editor: Timothy Cooke
Associate Editors: Robert Anderson, David Scott-Macnab, Casey Horton
Design: Wilson Design Associates
Picture Research: Jenny Speller, Adrian Bentley
Maps: Bill Lebihan
Index Editor: Kay Ollerenshaw

Library of Congress Cataloging-in-Publication Data

History of the modern world / [editor, Timothy Cooke].
    p. cm.
    Contents: v. 1. Origins of the modern world—v. 2. Religion and change in Europe—v. 3. Old and new worlds—v. 4. The Age of the Enlightenment—
v. 5. Revolution and change—v. 6. The changing balance of power—v. 7. World War I and its consequences—v. 8. World War II and the Cold War—
v. 9. The world today—v. 10. Index
    Includes bibliographical references and index.
    ISBN 0-7614-7147-2 (set).—ISBN 0-7614-7148-0 (v. 1).—ISBN 0-7614-7149-9 (v. 2).—ISBN 0-7614-7150-2 (v. 3).—ISBN 0-7614-7151-0 (v. 4).—
ISBN 0-7614-7152-9 (v. 5).—ISBN 0-7614-7153-7 (v. 6).—ISBN 0-7614-7154-5 (v. 7).—ISBN 0-7614-7155-3 (v. 8).—ISBN 0-7614-7156-1 (v. 9).—
ISBN 0-7614-7157-X (v. 10).
    1. World history Juvenile literature. I. Cooke, Timothy, 1961- .
D20.h544 1999
909.08—dc21
           99-14780
           CIP

ISBN 0-7614-7147-2 (set)
ISBN 0-7614-7153-7 (v. 6)

Printed and bound in Italy

07 06 05 04 03 02 01 00 7 6 5 4 3 2 1

History of the
Modern World

Volume 6

The Changing Balance of Power

Marshall Cavendish
New York • London • Toronto • Sydney

The Changing Balance of Powe

冨嶽三十六景 神奈川沖 浪裏

The Wave by Katsushika Hokusai, color woodcut, nineteenth century.

CONTENTS

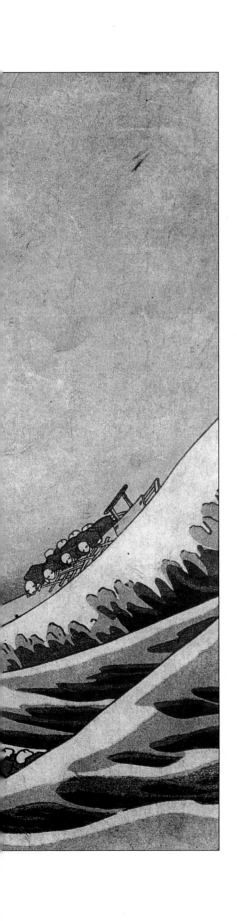

Introduction

The Changing Balance of Power tells the story of a rapidly changing world as the effects of the industrialization of western Europe and the United States were felt around the globe. Chapter one shows how the Ottoman Empire, which had long dominated the Middle East and southeastern Europe, declined under external pressures from hostile neighbors and the internal weakness of once-powerful institutions no longer suited to the modernizing world.

Chapters two, three, and four discuss political change in Mexico and South America, which freed themselves from European rule in a series of violent revolutions. The independent nations created, however, faced severe problems. Liberals and conservatives struggled for power and numerous countries evolved a tradition of military government. In Mexico, nearly a century of instability ended in revolution in 1910. The shadow of the United States fell over the entire region. Mexico fought unsuccessful border conflicts with its neighbor while the countries of South America found themselves unwillingly harnessed to the dominant U.S. economy.

China and Japan, too, felt the impact of the West, as explained in chapters five and six. China found its policy of isolation threatened by Europeans determined to establish trade links. The country was shaken by two great peasant rebellions, one inspired by Christianity, the other by protests against foreign influence. Japan, on the other hand, embraced western industrial techniques and methods, but on its own terms. Technological advances enabled Japan to win military victories first over China and then Russia at the end of the century.

As chapters seven and eight demonstrate, the continuing industrialization of the West brought constant change to everyday life, introducing new levels of material ownership and individual freedom for many. The excesses of industrial life, meanwhile, inspired the emergence of socialist movements that aspired to a more just society, as outlined in chapter nine. This volume's final chapter shows how developments such as the camera affected the arts, producing new forms of culture for an industrialized world.

Africa was rich in natural resources. Chapter ten explains how the countries of Europe used their military superiority to divide up the continent, seeking both those resources and national prestige. Chapter eleven describes a parallel process in the United States, where prosperity returned after the Civil War. An influx of immigrants prompted a westward expansion in search of land and raw materials. The victims here were the Native Americans. Their tragic fate was exemplified by the events at Wounded Knee in 1890.

The Editor

The Shrinking Ottoman World

The Decline of the Turkish Empire

At its greatest extent, in 1683, the chiefly Muslim empire ruled by the Ottoman dynasty stretched from the borders of present-day Iran in the east as far west as Algeria, from Hungary in the north to southern Arabia (*see 1:107*). The Ottomans had expanded from their homeland in central Asia to control the eastern Mediterranean and what is now called the Middle East. The Ottoman sultan was the temporal leader of the majority of the world's Muslims.

The eighteenth and nineteenth centuries, however, brought a slow decline that culminated in the final collapse of the empire in 1918, amid the peace settlements that ended World War I. The absence of imperial control has fueled ethnic and religious rivalries throughout the Middle East up to the present.

The Empire's Problems

Part of the Ottoman Empire's problems lay in the fact that it faced powerful enemies to the west, to the north, and to the east. Its expansion had been fiercely resisted by the Venetian Empire in the Mediterranean and

This photograph from around 1890 shows worshipers around a mosque. The Ottoman Empire was a theocracy dedicated to the preservation of the Islamic faith.

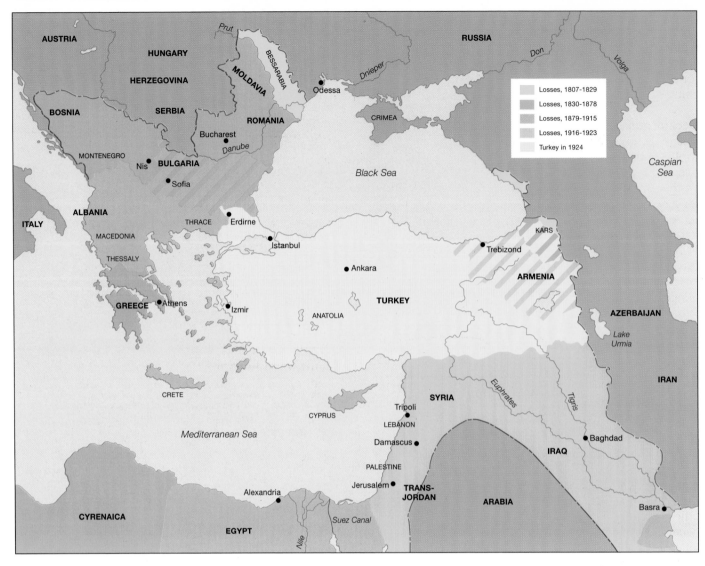

Losses, 1807–1829
Losses, 1830–1878
Losses, 1879–1915
Losses, 1916–1923
Turkey in 1924

This map of the Ottoman Empire shows the territory it lost during the nineteenth century.

the Habsburg dynasty in central Europe. In the east, the nationalistic Safavid dynasty of Iran practiced Shiite Islam. It rejected the authority of the Ottoman caliph, who led the Sunni branch of the faith (*see 1:99*). Although Venice was in steep decline by the early eighteenth century, another powerful long-term foe, the Russian Empire, emerged around the same time as a great threat.

The Ottoman sultan stood at the head of a theocratic government committed to the protection of Islam. In a theocracy, the state is run as an instrument of religion. The empire itself, however, was ethnically and religiously mixed: it contained Slavs, various Turkish groups, Kurds, and Arabs, and had a large Orthodox Christian population living mainly in Greece and the Balkans. The Ottomans solved this problem by maintaining an Islamic ruling class but allowing their subjects a relatively high degree of autonomy in communities called *millets*, which were divided along religious lines. The empire also tried to win the loyalty of its Christian populations by using

talented Christian converts to Islam in the service of the sultan. These converts contributed to a complex bureaucracy, run by a chief minister called the grand vizier, which efficiently administered and taxed the empire.

The bureaucracy also administered the remarkable Ottoman army, which might be called to defend any of the far-flung borders of the empire. Troops called janissaries—originally the sons of Christian subjects seized as tribute or as war booty—formed the elite infantry corps of the regular Ottoman army, which was supplemented by the forces of local nobles, called notables, who were rewarded for military service with grants of territory. Such an arrangement meant that power was never wholly centralized.

Military superiority convinced key elements of the Ottoman state, such as the janissaries, that they had little to learn from Europe. The Ottoman state remained assured of its own superiority and showed little interest in other ways of life in the seventeenth century. It knew nothing, for example, of the Scientific Revolution (*see 2:265*). The Ottoman isolation was perhaps typical of the attitudes developed by a large empire with a long tradition. The Chinese, for example, shared a similar view of other cultures (*see 3:523*).

Decline and Dilemmas

The seventeenth century saw clear setbacks for the empire. The Safavids of Iran almost overran the empire (*see 3:397*), and the Ottomans were unable to conclude their long naval war with Venice for control of the eastern Mediterranean. Then, in 1683, when the Ottomans attacked Vienna, capital of the Habsburg Empire, their troops were driven back. Ottoman forces never threatened central Europe again. Over the next hundred years, a series of wars against Russia, Venice, and Austria forced the Ottomans to surrender large sections of their European lands. The first to be taken were Hungary and Transylvania, by the Treaty of Belgrade in 1739.

As the Ottomans' international strength declined, so the empire's internal weaknesses grew. In many provinces, notables ruled virtually independently, finding popular support from populations who had grown disenchanted with centralized Ottoman rule. The notables seized taxes and disrupted food supplies to the empire's cities, where famine became a regular occurrence. The urban population became angry and violent, rioting and executing imperial officials.

At the heart of the Ottoman problem in the eighteenth and nineteenth centuries lay a dilemma that still affects some Islamic states today. In the face of the changing world around them, should the Ottomans try to maintain a conservative, Islamic way of life or should they modernize the empire along Western lines? Conservative elements in society, such as the janissaries and the ulema, the priests and scholars who led the Islamic faith, believed that the first option was better.

Conservative Forces

As the empire was an Islamic theocracy, religious leaders occupied a privileged place in society. In practice, the ulema controlled both education and justice. They did not have to pay taxes, and only they had the authority to dethrone a sultan—often at the request of the janissaries or the central bureaucracy—by issuing a *fatwa*, or decree, for his removal. The ulema were respected as the best-educated members of society. Any reforms in the administration of the empire, therefore, or any attempt to

This contemporary portrait shows Selim III, who many people see as the first of the Ottomans' modernizing reformers.

educate the mass of the people outside the traditions of Islam threatened to weaken their authority.

Echoing the West

A vogue for European culture began in the Tulip Period of 1717 to 1730. In an imitation of the French court at Versailles (*2:262*), the Ottoman ruling class built Western palaces, adopted European styles of dress, and began to grow tulips as a sign of their westernization. In 1727, the first Turkish printing press was founded, followed by the first artillery and naval schools, both intended to introduce European methods of warfare.

This detail from an eighteenth-century drawing shows a janissary officer in traditional uniform.

The influence of the West later itself became a problem, most importantly with the emergence of nationalist feeling in the Ottomans' European lands. Particularly in the Balkans, where loyalty to the empire had never been strong, the appeal of European ideas about democracy and national self-government grew among the Christian subjects of the empire.

In 1770, a Russian fleet wiped out the Ottoman navy at the Battle of Çesme. In 1774, at the treaty of Küçük-Kainardji, the Russians forced the empire to grant free navigation on the Black Sea, which for centuries had been considered an exclusively Ottoman region. Within twenty years, the Russians would control the whole of the sea's north coast. The Russians also claimed a protectorate over all of the Ottomans' Christian subjects.

Changes in Outlook

In 1789, the year the French Revolution began in Europe, a new sultan came to the Ottoman throne. Selim III (1761–1808) was determined to modernize the empire. Well educated, a talented poet and musician, Selim refused to be handicapped by tradition. Selim's own commitment to reform became apparent when he was one of the first world rulers to recognize the new French republic.

In Europe, the impetus for revolution had come from the people. In Ottoman Turkey, change came from above and innovation sprang from the sultan himself. The impulse for reform was not a simple imitation of the West, however. The Ottoman rulers had come to realize that reform was the only way to preserve the empire.

In an effort to circumvent the conservatism of the janissaries, Selim III created a new army on Western lines. Numbering around 10,000 men, this force learned tactics from advisers sent by European powers who were eager to establish friendly relations with the Ottomans. European advisers also oversaw the establishment of modern arms factories and military schools. The sultan funded his reforms with an improved taxation system.

Selim's reforms made him enemies among the janissaries and ulema, who dubbed him the Infidel Sultan. At the same time, notables challenged imperial power in southeastern Europe, Anatolia, and Arabia. Napoleon led a French military expedition into Egypt while, in an attempt to undermine the empire, Russian, Austrian, and French agitators stirred up nationalist feelings in the Balkans, where revolution began in Serbia in 1804. Selim was overthrown by conservatives in 1807, imprisoned, and later killed. Although his reforms were largely abandoned, they had changed the empire for good by increasing its contact with the West.

A New Reformer

Selim's successor, Mahmut II (1785–1839), faced desperate problems. Central authority was decaying. Russia invaded Ottoman territory in the Balkans in 1806; Britain invaded Egypt the next year. Only after the Ottomans made peace with both opponents was Mahmut able to concentrate on reform.

Like Selim, the sultan saw reform of the army as the way to reestablish Ottoman power. Unlike Selim, however, he portrayed his reforms not as Western innovations but as a return to Ottoman military tradition, which won him the support of the ulema. In 1826, Mahmut announced plans to form a European-style army. The janissaries of Istanbul mutinied against the plan but had no allies: the sultan had them mas-

This early-twentieth-century photograph shows the Bosporus, the channel linking the Black Sea and the Mediterranean. The strait was controlled by the Ottoman capital, Istanbul (formerly Constantinople).

sacred, ending the influence of the janissaries for ever. Ottoman historians called the massacre the "auspicious incident."

Trained by mainly European advisers, including the future German general Helmuth von Moltke (*see 5:663*), the new army prompted modernization in tax collection to fund it and higher education to train officers. Mahmut opened a modern medical school, abolished the last traces of feudalism, and started the first Turkish newspaper. The sultan also began to undermine the power of the ulema and centralize it in an efficient bureaucracy.

Mahmut's attempts to reimpose centralized rule on the empire met with great resistance. In 1821, Greek patriots rose in revolt against their Ottoman rulers to establish a Greek homeland in a rebellion inspired by the nationalism then becoming

Mahmut II wears traditional clothing in this portrait. In 1828, the sultan symbolized the respectability of change by replacing the Ottomans' traditional formal turban with a red, tasseled hat, the fez.

This photograph shows a steep street in Istanbul around 1900. Most of the pedestrians are wearing Western-style clothes.

pressure from Europeans. After a failed occupation of Egypt by Napoleon at the start of the century, the French returned to begin the conquest of Algeria in 1832; in 1881, they established a protectorate over neighboring Tunisia.

On the Arabian Peninsula, meanwhile, a tribal people called the Wahhabi exercised local dominance. Strict Muslims who came to the fore in the eighteenth century, the Wahhabi followed the Saudi dynasty, which originated from Nejd in central Arabia. The Wahhabi mounted a serious challenge to Ottoman authority at the start of the century. They occupied Mecca, the holy city of Islam, until they were suppressed by Egyptian forces fighting for the sultan. In 1824, the Saudis rebelled against imperial authority again. They captured the city of Riyadh, which became the capital of a new Arabian kingdom.

Egypt's Independence

The Egyptians themselves represented the most enduring challenge to Ottoman rule in the region. After the brief French occupation in 1799, the Egyptians rose up against the Ottoman viceroy in 1805 and installed Muhammad Ali in his place. A soldier, the new leader set about undermining the landowning Mamluks, many of whom he had executed, and establishing a monopoly over property and agriculture. Muhammad Ali wanted to modernize Egypt on Western lines. He encouraged industrialization, though with limited success, and reformed the army, bringing in Ottoman and French officers to run it.

Muhammad Ali led a military expansion of Egypt, challenging the Wahhabi in Arabia and conquering Sudan, where he took control of the lucrative slave trade. The Egyptians achieved other military successes in Crete and southern Greece before, in 1831, Muhammad Ali launched his most audacious move. He invaded the wheat- and timber-rich lands of Syria and threatened Istanbul itself. When Mahmut II died in 1839, the empire seemed on the verge of collapse until the European powers intervened to reestablish Ottoman rule of Syria. In 1841 the sultan was forced to proclaim Muhammad Ali's family the hereditary rulers of Egypt.

The decline of imperial control over North Africa and the Middle East had lasting effects. It reduced Ottoman access to the Mediterranean and the Red Sea. It also undermined the sultan's claim to be caliph of all Muslims. Maintaining the sultan's supremacy was an important policy of what was called the Pan-Islamic move-

apparent elsewhere in Europe (*see 5:610*). Idealistic Europeans flocked to their cause. The Ottomans subdued the revolt, but Russia, France, and Britain intervened. In 1827, their combined fleets destroyed the Ottoman navy at the Battle of Navarino and forced the sultan to concede independence to a small Greek state. The interference of the West set a pattern for the future. Later in the century, Western intervention overturned Ottoman victories against the Serbs and the Montenegrins. In 1829, defeat by the Russians forced the Ottomans to surrender territory in the Balkans and Anatolia. In 1830, they recognized the autonomy of Serbia.

While nationalist feelings stirred the empire's non-Muslim population, developments in the Middle East and North Africa reflected discontent among the Ottomans' Muslim subjects. The countries of the North African littoral, or coast, came under ment, which emerged to promote Islamic unity as a means of strengthening the Muslim world.

The Tanzimat

Mahmut was succeeded by his sons Abdül-mecid, who ruled from 1839 to 1861, and Abdülaziz, who ruled from 1861 to 1876. The two rulers implemented a series of reforms known as the Tanzimat. The most famous reform, the 1839 Edict of Gulhane, established the equality of all subjects as the basis of Ottoman law and government. A later pronouncement guaranteed equal opportunity in employment.

Other reforms established a universal system of education, free from religious control, with a curriculum that included science and philosophy. A system of state courts was established, separate from the religious control of the ulema. In 1876, a constitution maintained the sultan's position as a despotic ruler, even though it also created independent judges, guaranteed freedom of speech and religion, and promised to protect private property.

Some historians dismiss the reforms of the Tanzimat as Ottoman attempts to win Western support by promising improved conditions for the empire's Christians. The promised equality, they point out, did not always exist in practice. Non-Muslims still paid higher taxes, for example. The gap between promise and reality allowed the Russians to reassert their position as defenders of the empire's Christian peoples, as established at Küçük-Kainardji in 1774. Russia itself had ambitions on Constantinople, now Istanbul, which guarded the entrance to the Black Sea. Russian control of the city would guarantee vital access to the Mediterranean. Constantinople also had a spiritual importance to Russians as the center of Orthodox Christianity.

Quarrels in the Balkans

Russian ambition led to war with the Ottomans in the Crimean War (1853–1856), when France and Great Britain aided the empire. Apparently unable to protect itself, the Ottoman Empire was by now mocked in the West as the "sick man of Europe." In

The minarets of a mosque tower above Nicosia, in Cyprus. Control of the island, seized by the British in 1878, is still disputed between Christians and Muslims.

A French magazine illustration from the end of the nineteenth century shows officers in the reformed Ottoman army, which had adopted Western uniforms, weapons, and tactics in an effort to resist European intervention in the empire.

the 1870s, discontent and nationalism led to uprisings in Bosnia-Herzegovina and Bulgaria. In the latter, bands of Ottoman refugees and military deserters massacred large numbers of Bulgarian peasants. Ottoman attempts to suppress the risings led to war with Serbia and Montenegro. Taking advantage of the upheaval, the Russians declared war again in 1877.

In 1878, representatives of all the European powers gathered at Berlin to seek a solution to the quarrels in the Balkans: between the great powers, between Christians and Muslim, between Slavs and non-Slavs. Eventually the rivalries in the region were to contribute to the outbreak of World War I (*see 7:876*).

The Treaty of Berlin brought a measure of peace and stability to the region, but it also underlined the fragility of Turkey's presence in Europe. It confirmed the independence of Serbia, Montenegro, and Romania and created the new state of Bulgaria. Russia claimed land in Asia Minor, while Austria-Hungary took control of Bosnia-Herzegovina. The same year, Great Britain occupied the Ottoman island of Cyprus in the Mediterranean. The Ottomans were also forced to repay massive international debts. A European agency even took control over Ottoman finances.

Abdülhamid's Tyranny

The Treaty of Berlin signaled the beginning of the end of the Ottoman Empire in Europe. It also brought the era of reform to a halt. A new sultan, Abdülhamid II, dismissed parliament and abandoned the 1876 constitution. Turkey fell under an absolute tyranny. Ironically, the reforms of the Tanzimat made the tyranny more effective, since they had already increased the centralization of power. The constitution confirmed the supremacy of the sultan's will.

Now, even the word *freedom* was removed from dictionaries, for example, and electricity was banned as a Western invention. The telegraph and railroads, on the other hand, were useful weapons for Abdülhamid to monopolize his power. He established an extensive spy system to suppress opposition. From 1894 to 1896, he launched a brutal repression of the Armenian peoples of the Caucasus, in which 50,000 Armenian Christians died. Europeans dubbed him the Red Sultan.

Poverty and the denial of legal freedoms went hand in hand. In the European lands still under Ottoman rule, economic decline destroyed people's sense of living together in a community. In 1881, a French writer who was visiting the region described how the roads were not safe to travel: "Refugees from all the countries lost by the empire and driven to crime by misery scour the roads at will… at the gates of Izmit (not far from the capital) market gardeners are robbed and murdered."

Turkish Nationalism

Opposition to the sultan could mean imprisonment without trial, exile, or even death. Even so, some continued to struggle for reform to preserve the empire. Among them were the Young Ottomans, a group of intellectuals who argued that the empire need not adopt Western traditions but should encourage Ottoman nationalism and draw on Islamic precedent to establish an assembly that could limit the will of the

sultan. Abdülhamid had the organization's leaders executed or exiled.

The Young Ottomans were the forerunners of the Young Turks. The Young Turks, though never a formal group or movement, shared a belief that the tyranny of Abdülhamid and European interventions were threatening the existence of the empire. The Young Turks were not liberals—they would launch their own brutal repression of the Armenians in World War I, for example—but they saw a need for industrialization, education, and secularization to strengthen the empire.

The Young Turks were inspired by a new force, Turkish nationalism. For centuries, the Turks had subdugated their sense of being Turkish to the sense of belonging to the empire. They saw themselves as Ottomans or Muslims rather than Turks. The name Turkey was not used until the first decade of the twentieth century and did not become the official name of the country until 1921, after the end of the empire.

The seeds of Turkish nationalism had been planted by intellectuals in the nineteenth century. In 1897, the poet Mehmet Emin declared: "I am a Turk, my faith and my race are mighty." Within a decade, a

This British cartoon from around 1900 is entitled *Turkey Gobblers and their Rations*. Crowding around Turkey are Britain, shown as John Bull standing on the islands of Malta and Corfu, and holding the lion of Egypt; Austria, shown as the double-headed imperial eagle; and Russia, depicted as a bear padding through the Black Sea.

This undated lithograph shows the Ottoman flag flying over an Egyptian scene. In reality, the Ottomans lost control of Egypt first to the Egyptians themselves and later to Britain. 735

Wearing Western suits and ties with their Turkish fezzes, two Young Turk reformers pose for the camera in the late nineteenth century. On the left is Kemal Atatürk, later a great Turkish general and statesman.

host of nationalist movements emerged that the sultan could not suppress.

Strict censorship failed to contain the spread of nationalist newspapers and journals. Illegal political movements encouraged the cause, led by the Committee of Union and Progress, whose members were forced into exile in Paris. The spirit of renewal and revolution infected even the army, where groups of nationalists plotted to overthrow the tyranny of the sultan.

In July 1908, a Young Turk revolt broke out in Monastir, calling for the restoration of the constitution. Discontented troops backed the rising, and Abdülhamid had no choice but to give in. The sultan restored the constitution, lifted all press censorship, ended police espionage, and called elections to a new parliament. In 1876, the parliament had sworn allegiance to the sultan; in 1908, the sultan swore allegiance to parliament and the constitution. A year later, Abdülhamid was deposed. The Young Turks effectively ruled the empire.

Reform had come too late to save the empire, however. In 1914, nationalism in the Balkans provided the spark that began World War I. At the end of the conflict that followed, the Ottoman Empire would disappear from the map forever (see 7:906).

Revolution in Mexico

A Century's Struggle for Stability

At the start of the nineteenth century, Mexico was a vast territory that stretched from present-day Colorado, Nevada, and California in the north to Guatemala, in Central America. The population of about six million, made up largely of farmers and peasants, was ruled by the Spanish, as Mexico had been since the sixteenth century (*see 3:343*). The early nineteenth century saw the Mexicans throw off Spanish rule. Independence did not bring peace or stability, however. Relations with the United States and internal politics made the period one of upheaval for many Mexicans.

The Stirrings of Revolution

Mexican society at the start of the nineteenth century was dominated by people of European descent, either Spanish-born peninsulares or Mexican-born criollos, or Creoles. Mexico's native Indians had little political power. Separate legal codes rein-

forced the superiority of the peninsulares over the criollos. The criollo majority grew increasingly frustrated by their lack of power and increasingly resentful of the dominance of distant Spain. Unlike the case in other South American countries, however, the first spark of rebellion came from outside the criollo elite. On September 16, 1810, Miguel Hidalgo, a criollo priest whose bishop had sent him to work in the small Indian village of Dolores, called for a rebellion against the Spanish. Embittered by two years of drought and famine, Hidalgo's peasant followers killed peninsulares and captured a number of provincial towns before some 80,000 rebels marched on Mexico City itself. Royalist armies crushed the uprising in January 1811. Hidalgo was captured and executed.

From around 1815, agitation for independence increased in Mexico. The chance for a breakthrough came in January 1820

Armed revolutionaries guard a train during the Mexican Revolution, which broke out in 1910. Control of the railroads was vital to both sides as the Mexican landscape made it difficult to move troops or supplies in any other way.

A statue in Guadalajara shows Miguel Hidalgo breaking free of a pair of chains. In 1810, Hidalgo, a parish priest, became the first Mexican to call for independence from Spain, Indian rights, and the redistribution of land. Hidalgo and his followers launched a rebellion against the government. The priest was captured and executed in 1811.

from an unlikely source: the Spanish army. A mutiny in Cádiz, led by officers demanding more pay, weakened the Spanish monarchy at home and in America.

The next year, a coalition of Mexican rebels met with a Spanish representative to devise the Plan of Iguala, by which Mexico would become an independent empire, ruled by a Spanish emperor. In fact, after a revision of the plan, the first emperor was Agustín de Iturbide, a Mexican elected by a congress. Catholicism would continue as the official religion, guaranteeing the continuing power of the Catholic Church (*see 3:352*). Most important, all Mexicans—peninsulares, criollos, and Indians—were to be equal before the law. Spain refused to accept the plan, but with no money, provisions, or troops, the Spanish in Mexico had no way of opposing it.

The Mexican Republic

In December 1822, after Iturbide dismissed congress to rule through a military junta, an ambitious army colonel, Antonio López de Santa Anna (1794–1876), proclaimed Mexico a republic. The charismatic soldier won the backing of the army and, on March 19, 1823, the emperor abdicated. The same ability to inspire loyalty would eventually lead to Santa Anna's serving as president four times between 1833 and 1855.

The proclamation of the republic opened a division among Mexico's rulers that shaped the rest of the century. While most of the peninsulares returned to Spain, the criollo elite split into conservative and liberal camps. The conservatives wanted to preserve the social hierarchy implicit in the idea of a monarchy. They sought the continuing power and authority of the Catholic Church and the army and the suppression of Mexico's Indians. Liberals, meanwhile, resembled European liberals in their belief in individual rights and less state intervention (*see 5:610*). Neither group, however, paid much attention to the native population. They clashed mainly over the role of the Catholic Church, which liberals wanted to see separated from the state. For its part, the church refused to recognize the republic until after 1835, weakening its position within Mexico.

War with the United States

After independence, Mexico's government alternated between conservatives and liberals, leaving the country in chaos. The Indian population became increasingly angry as their living standards failed to improve. The country had little money. Potentially lucrative industries such as mining had relied to a large extent on the expertise of peninsulares who had now departed. The money the government could raise, mainly from customs duties, was not enough even to pay the army. To support the military, Mexico had to take out high-interest loans with foreign governments. Nevertheless, Santa Anna was able to defeat both an attempted Spanish reconquest in 1829 and the French seizure of Veracruz in 1838, during which Santa Anna was wounded and lost a leg.

The Texas Question

In 1835, an uprising broke out in Texas. Although Texas was still part of Mexico, some 30,000 U.S. citizens had settled the desolate region. When Santa Anna, now president, tried to limit the rights of Mexican states, the Texans declared independence. Santa Anna marched to San Antonio in February 1836 and defeated a Texan garrison at the renowned siege of the Alamo. Santa Anna's subsequent execution of his prisoners inspired the Texan rallying cry, "Remember the Alamo." In April, at the Battle of San Jacinto, the Texans narrowly defeated Santa Anna. Although Mexico refused to acknowledge Texan independence, it did not try to recapture its territory.

The Maya Indians of the southern Mexican state of Yucatán, meanwhile, rose up

This portrait shows Antonio López de Santa Anna. Santa Anna's magnetic personality dominated Mexican politics for some twenty years, but he is best remembered for his pride and lack of principles.

against their criollo governors. The Mexican army, occupied in suppressing the Maya revolt and other rebellions that broke out across the country, could not resist the United States' annexation of Texas in 1845. When Santa Anna appeared willing to negotiate with the Americans, he was overthrown and the army assumed power.

In the United States, the doctrine of Manifest Destiny was at its height. Most Americans sincerely believed in the right of the United States to occupy all of North America (*see 5:652*). When the United States tried to extend the Texas boundary from the Rio Grande to the Nueces River in April 1846, it sent troops to occupy the disputed land. Mexican troops defended what was technically Mexican soil, but the United States declared war.

American troops easily captured what are now the states of New Mexico and California. Zachary Taylor, later president of the United States, defeated Santa Anna in the Battle of Buena Vista in February 1847. Another U.S. force captured Mexico City itself in September. Santa Anna went into exile. The peace treaty turned over to the United States half of Mexico's territory, including what became California, Nevada,

This contemporary German print shows U.S. forces commanded by General Winfield Scott attacking Mexico City in 1847.

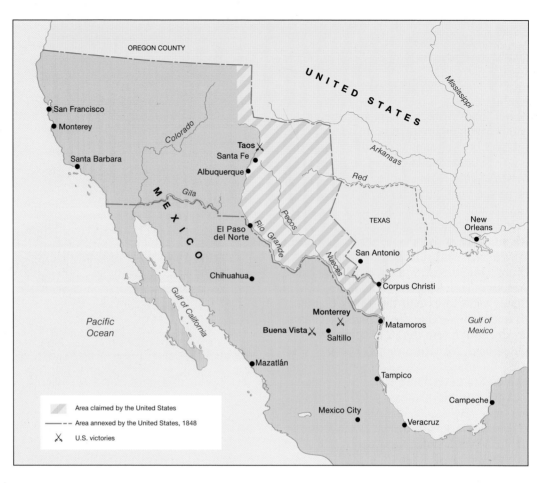

This map shows the changing boundaries of Mexico in the nineteenth century and the vast area lost to the United States following the war of 1848.

Utah, most of Arizona, parts of Wyoming, Colorado, and New Mexico. The United States paid $15 million for the land. In 1853, Mexico's boundaries changed significantly for the last time when the United States paid another $10 million for land south of the Gila River in what was called the Gadsden Purchase.

The Age of Reform

The money Mexico received for its land helped strengthen the army, which temporarily suppressed the Indian rebellions. Meanwhile, the liberals gained the upper hand in government. The easy victory of the United States had shocked many people into believing that Mexico's only hope of survival lay in fundamental reform.

The man who steered that reform was a Zapotec Indian from the southern state of Oaxaca, Benito Juárez (1806–1872). A lawyer dedicated to defending Indian rights, Juárez was Mexico's minister of justice. He and other liberals promoted the idea of La Reforma, or the Reform, a program that aimed to free Mexico from its colonial past and create a secular state of farms and small businesses guided by principles of equality.

In 1857, Mexico adopted a new liberal constitution that weakened the power of the army and the church and reduced the privileges of officers and priests. Conservative hostility to the constitution led to a bloody civil war, which the liberals eventually won in December 1860, with moral and diplomatic support from the United States. The following year, Juárez was elected as Mexico's first civilian president.

Napoleon III

Juárez inherited a country bankrupted by the civil war. He could not meet Mexico's foreign debt repayments. Claiming to be recovering unpaid loans, the ambitious Napoleon III of France sent troops to invade Mexico in 1862 (*see 5:657*). Juárez escaped to the countryside.

Napoleon intended to use Mexico as a base to establish a French sphere of influence in *Latin America*, a term that first appeared around this time. Napoleon reintroduced the monarchy, making the Habsburg archduke Maximilian of Austria and his Belgian wife, Charlotte, emperor and empress of Mexico in 1864. Maximilian was well intentioned but politically naive. He tried to befriend both the liberals and conservatives but lost the support of both by a series of clumsy political maneuvers.

Juárez's supporters inflicted several defeats on Maximilian's troops. In February 1866, facing criticism at home and from the United States, Napoleon abandoned

Maximilian and began to withdraw his troops. Empress Charlotte, touring Europe to rally support, lapsed into insanity. Maximilian was executed by Mexican troops in May 1867. The idea of a Mexican monarchy died with him.

The Monroe Doctrine

Napoleon's venture was possible only because the United States was distracted by the Civil War (1861–1865). The French move violated the principles of the Monroe Doctrine, proclaimed by President James Monroe in 1823 (*see 5:647*). American governments have used the doctrine to justify their actions in Latin America up to the present day. It pledged U.S. support for any New World country threatened by a nation from outside the Americas. It effectively gave the United States the right to interfere in the affairs of weaker nations in the hemisphere. The United States had used the doctrine to justify its war with Mexico and annexation of Mexican territories.

Porfirio Díaz

The civil wars of Maximilian's reign had cost some 50,000 lives and left the country as poor as ever. When Juárez returned to power, he set out to repair the economy, encouraging investment from America and Europe. A railroad was built to join Mexico

el partido
ha guiado al
pueblo por la via
del progreso

Benito Juarez

This modest house in Oaxaca was the home of Benito Juárez. Today it is a museum in his memory.

This bust of Benito Juárez in Mexico City includes one of his slogans: "The party has guided the people along the path of progress."

This church stands in Cuernavaca in Morelos, the state where Zapata led a peasant revolt. The Catholic Church won many adherents among Mexico's Indians, who often adapted it to their traditional beliefs.

The Mexican Indians

The political changes of the nineteenth century left untouched the largest section of Mexican society, the native Indians. Living largely as rural farmers, the Indians played little part in Mexican independence and gained little benefit from it. Their lives remained hard; the Indians found compensation in the Catholic religion, imported by European missionaries since the sixteenth century, which the Indians often adapted to their own traditional beliefs.

Rather than political change, the enduring concern of the Indians remained land. Skilled farmers, the Indians needed land to grow the corn and other staples that formed the basis of their diet. The creation of large estates, called haciendas, by the criollo elite often deprived villages of their traditional lands. Indian discontent mani-fested itself in frequent uprisings and in the banditry that plagued the countryside. The constitution of 1857, although it sought a redistribution of church and public land, left the Indians just as badly off, despite the presidency of Benito Juárez, an Indian from Oaxaca.

During the rule of Porfirio Díaz, the Indians suffered under the dictator's determined repression of all sources of possible discontent and opposition. The Yaqui Indians, for example, were shipped as cheap labor to the sisal plantations of the Yucatán or the tobacco plantations of the Oaxaca Valley. By the end of the nineteenth century, Indian discontent had grown to the stage where calls for land reform by Zapata and Pancho Villa won thousands of Indian supporters to fight in the 1910 revolution.

City to the port of Veracruz. Telegraph lines ran along new roads. Mexico adopted metric weights and measures, while Juárez also extended public education.

Juárez died in 1872. His successor was overthrown four years later by Porfirio Díaz (1830–1915). Díaz was a mestizo, of mixed Indian and Spanish descent, born to a poor family in Oaxaca. A professional soldier renowned for clean living. Díaz had been Juárez's most successful general in the war against Maximilian. Díaz had since twice run against Juárez for president, though they shared many similar opinions.

In 1876, having organized a rebel army in the United States, Díaz marched on Mexico City and installed himself as president, an office he held for some thirty-five years. Although he retained the appearances of democratic government, such as elections, Díaz ruled as a caudillo, a Spanish word that refers to a dictator who gains political power by means of personal charisma, often after having led armies during wartime.

The Pax Porfiriana

Combining strong leadership and political stability, Díaz's rule became known as Pax Porfiriana, or Porfirio's peace. Díaz encouraged foreign investment, allowing American and British companies to own Mexico's oilfields, mines, and public utilities. New railroads enabled a dramatic increase in the mining of copper, zinc, and lead. In agriculture, cash crops for export such as coffee and sugarcane stimulated the rural economy. Large haciendas, or estates, were created from land previously owned by the church or by Indians.

The Pax Porfiriana did not benefit all Mexicans. Slogans such as "bread or the club" summed up Díaz's straightforward policy of social discipline: following his policies brought rewards but resisting brought punishment, such as enforced military conscription. Díaz's power rested on making support for his system in the people's self-interest. He made the church and army part of his regime rather than its opponents, thus undoing some of the effects of Juárez's reforms. He used gifts of land to reward supporters and U.S. investors. So powerful was U.S. influence in Mexico that Díaz is said to have exclaimed: "Poor Mexico, so far from God and so close to the United States!"

Díaz won much praise for his economic achievements, but Mexico's wealth and stability were deceptive. They depended on Díaz himself. As the dictator became less popular, discontent surfaced as Indian

This postcard, issued in 1910, shows Mexican president Porfirio Díaz in military uniform. A year later, Díaz was forced to step down.

peasants, deprived of their land, attacked landowners and students demonstrated against the dictatorship. An anarchist group, Regeneration, called for civil liberties, land reform in favor of Mexicans and Indians over foreigners, and improved conditions for workers. Díaz used the army to suppress strikes in the textile and copper-mining industries. In response to pressure, however, the president hinted in a press interview that he would welcome the creation of an opposition party to contend the presidential election of 1910.

The 1910 Mexican Revolution

Díaz's main opponent in the 1910 election was Francisco Madero (1873–1913), an intellectual from one of Mexico's richest landowning families. Seeing food prices

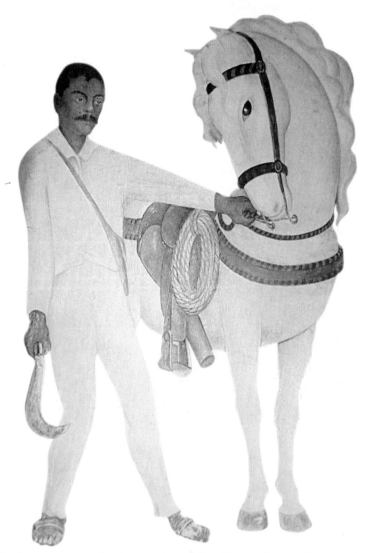

A detail from a mural painted by the famous Mexican artist Diego Rivera in the 1920s shows the rebel leader Emiliano Zapata.

Madero's call for revolution coincided with the emergence of two strong rebel leaders among Mexico's Indians. Francisco Villa, usually called Pancho Villa (1878–1923), and Emiliano Zapata (1879–1919) wanted more land for their people. They organized separate Indian revolts, Villa in the northern state of Chihuahua and Zapata in Morelos, south of Mexico City.

In February 1911, Madero left his base in Texas and crossed into Chihuahua, where he replaced Villa as leader of the rebels. The United States, which had given its tacit support to Madero, sent 20,000 troops to the Mexican border and warships to major ports. As the Mexican army proved ineffectual against the rebels, Díaz's supporters realized that he was fatally weakened. They suggested a compromise: Díaz would leave the country and Madero would call free elections. In return, Madero would disarm the rebels. On May 25, Díaz resigned and set sail for Paris.

Madero's Presidency

Madero was elected president in October 1911 in Mexico's first free election. It soon became apparent, however, that he was powerless to prevent peasant uprisings from breaking out throughout the country. In Morelos, Zapata rejected Madero's presidency and continued his fight against the landowners. He called on any peasant who had a title to land to reoccupy and defend it, with violence if necessary. Zapata also demanded that one-third of every large hacienda be given to local peasants.

With numerous uprisings and different groups fighting for power, Madero found it increasingly difficult to keep control. His position became even more vulnerable

rise while the rural and urban standard of living both fell, Madero originally decided to run for election as vice president. When Díaz had him jailed, however, Madero turned to rebellion. He called for a citizens' uprising and went into exile in Texas.

Rebel sharpshooters take shelter behind a wall during a battle with government troops in the 1910 revolution. The uprising cost the lives of a million Mexicans, most of them rural peasants.

when he alienated his main ally, the United States, by introducing a tax on oil production. Meanwhile, an army general called Victoriano Huerta (1854–1916) emerged to put down various peasant revolts and establish himself as the strongman of Mexican politics. On February 18, 1913, with the backing of the United States and the Mexican army, he staged a coup. Huerta's forces bombarded Mexico City for ten days, causing a high number of civilian casualties, before Madero was arrested and, shortly after, murdered.

Huerta in Power

While Huerta declared himself provisional president, Mexico's chaos continued. Zapata and Villa continued to fight for land for the peasants while anti-Huerta forces combined to bring down the government on the grounds that it was unconstitutional. General Venustiano Carranza, a state governor and Madero supporter, called for Huerta's overthrow and a return to constitutional government. The anti-Huerta forces divided into different armies. The Division of the North, commanded by Pancho Villa, attracted many Indian recruits with the rebel leader's radical social plans for land redistribution.

The United States and the Revolution

The warring factions all knew that they would have to deal with Washington if they were to successfully gain power. The United States' overriding concern was the reestablishment of stability to protect American investment in Mexico. President Woodrow Wilson disliked Huerta and increasingly supported Carranza. On a flimsy excuse, when Huerta refused to apologize for the arrest of U.S. sailors by Mexican officials, Wilson sent troops to occupy the Mexican port of Veracruz.

American troops took control of Veracruz on April 21, 1914. The port was essential to Huerta for its customshouse, which was a major source of government revenue. The United States remained in Veracruz until November, however, blocking Huerta's access to those funds and severely weakening his position. As Zapata and Villa made military gains, Huerta lost control of the country. In July 1914 he went into exile.

The Struggle for Power Continues

Huerta's departure did not end the war. As soon as Carranza declared himself president in July 1914, he was deserted by both Villa and Zapata. After a series of defeats

American sailors return to their ships after capturing Veracruz and handing it over to the U.S. Army in 1914.

745

PROCLAMATION
$5,000⁰⁰ REWARD

FRANCISCO (PANCHO) VILLA

ALSO $1,000. REWARD FOR ARREST OF CANDELARIO CERVANTES, PABLO LOPEZ, FRANCISCO BELTRAN, MARTIN LOPEZ

ANY INFORMATION LEADING TO HIS APPREHENSION WILL BE REWARDED.

CHIEF OF POLICE
Columbus
New Mexico

MARCH 9, 1916

A wanted poster from Columbus, New Mexico, offers a reward for information on the whereabouts of Pancho Villa after his 1916 raid on the town.

by Carranza's forces, Villa fled to the northern mountains. In an effort to demonstrate his continuing power in the north, Villa started to halt trains near the border and kill any Americans on board.

In 1916, Villa crossed the border into Columbus, New Mexico, where he killed sixteen Americans. Outraged, Woodrow Wilson sent General John Joseph Pershing to Mexico to find Villa, but Villa knew the barren territory and was popular among its Indian inhabitants. Pershing left in 1917 without catching Villa, who was later pardoned by the Mexican government in return for a promise to retire from politics. In Morelos, meanwhile, Zapata continued to fight government forces until he was betrayed and killed in 1919.

The 1917 Constitution

In 1917, Carranza's government introduced a constitution that incorporated many of the aspirations of revolutionaries such as Villa and Zapata. It proposed land reform, the establishment of civil liberties, and active government intervention to improve the lives of all Mexicans. It also limited foreign influence in Mexico.

In 1920, Carranza was overthrown by General Alvaro Obregón after failing to institute further social reforms. Obregón came to power determined to rehabilitate his country after a decade of conflict that had left more than a million Mexicans dead. He launched a program of reform intended to bring peace to the country and offer hope for the future (*see 7:971*).

Revolution in South America

Breaking the Chains of Colonial Rule

When the nineteenth century began, Spain and Portugal had ruled South America for more than 300 years. The continent was largely stable and peaceful. Any rumblings of revolt were easily quashed before they could pose a serious threat to Iberian control of the region. Dramatic change was on the horizon, however. A series of reforms introduced by Spain's Bourbon rulers early in the eighteenth century aimed to tighten Spanish control over the colonies. Instead, the reforms achieved the opposite, creating resentment among Spain's colonial subjects that eventually led to revolution.

Bourbon Reforms
During the eighteenth century, Spain suffered great setbacks in Europe. The rise of France and Britain, in particular, helped lessen Spain's wealth, power, and prestige (*see 4:467*). As a result, Spain's Bourbon rulers saw their colonies as increasingly important to Spanish national interests. Specifically, they regarded the colonies as a means of raising income. The Bourbons initiated a series of reforms to increase tax revenue from Latin America and stimulate the Spanish economy. The reforms were designed to achieve this end by reorganizing the colonies' administrations and by controlling their commercial output.

In 1717, Spain overhauled the administration of its South American colonies. A viceroy in Lima, Peru, had previously governed all of Spanish South America except Venezuela, which, like Mexico, was part of the viceroyalty of New Spain (*see 3:346*). The viceroy's power was considerably reduced when Spain created a second viceroyalty, called New Granada, compris-

This contemporary painting shows the Spanish signing the treaty that accepted the independence of Venezuela in August 1823.

747

This bust in Chile commemorates the early patriot Bernardo O'Higgins, who became the country's first head of state after liberation. O'Higgins's name came from his father, a Spanish soldier with Irish roots.

American ports allowed to trade directly across the Atlantic. The Bourbons forced Latin America to import Spanish products, while at the same time forbidding the colonies from producing anything that might compete with the imports, such as wheat and olive oil.

In return, Spain increased the number of licensed colonial trading ports and gave the colonies favorable tax incentives. The Spanish called their commercial reforms *un comercio libre y protegido*, or "free trade under the protection of the state." The policy did much to stimulate the colonial economy, but its main intention was always to protect the interests of Spain.

Growing Dissatisfaction with Spain

Whatever benefits the Bourbon reforms brought to the colonies, they created growing resentment. For one thing, the Spanish economy was unable to satisfy Latin American demand for its produce, making local criollos even more unhappy that their economy was dominated by "foreign" peninsulares. Priests were angered by the forced sale of church lands, and wealthy criollos begrudged Spanish pressure to pay for distant European wars.

South America's Indian communities traditionally played little role in politics, but even they were affected by increased sales taxes and the higher tributes payable to the Spanish crown. Anti-Spanish feeling started to break out into riots across the continent.

Events elsewhere in the world stimulated further unrest. The American Revolutionary War of 1776 and its rejection of British colonial rule had a profound impact on Latin America. So, too, did the French Revolution of 1789 in its overthrow of a decadent monarchy and aristocracy. No less influential were general Enlightenment ideas about equality, liberty, and freedom from state control (*see 4:471*). Even closer to home, Latin Americans were astonished when black revolutionaries in Haiti won independence for their country in 1804, making it only the second fully independent nation in the Americas, after the United States (*see 3:386*).

The South American Officer Corps

Among the South Americans most affected by revolutionary events elsewhere in the world were army officers. These men were largely criollos who found their paths to senior government positions blocked by peninsulares and turned to the army as a means of self-advancement. The Spanish crown granted criollos many privileges to attract them to the officer corps of the

ing Colombia, Ecuador, Venezuela, and Panama. In 1776, a further viceroyalty was set up at Buenos Aires to control Argentina, Uruguay, Paraguay, and Bolivia.

The creation of the new viceroyalties effectively limited the power of any single viceroy. As a further step to ensure their control over the region, the Bourbons filled key government posts with officials sent out from Europe. This policy created great tension and deepened social divisions between the peninsulares, the people who were sent out from Spain, and the criollos, who were of European descent but had been born in South America.

In the field of commerce, Spain enforced strict controls over the number of Latin

army, exempting them from most offenses under civil law. This marked the beginning of the special officer class that has often dominated Latin American politics ever since, closely guarding its privileges. These officers were a potential source of unrest, as criollos in general tended to be deeply disenchanted with Spanish colonial rule.

Dramatic Events in Europe

The first moves toward independence in South America came in Venezuela, where a patriot called Francisco de Miranda (1750–1816) led a rebellion in 1806. Spanish rule was strong enough to suppress the uprising, but its power was about to be severely undermined. The immediate cause was Napoleon Bonaparte's sweeping conquests in western Europe (*see 5:598*).

In 1807, Napoleon occupied Portugal, forcing the Portuguese royal family to flee to Brazil. The following year, he invaded Spain, imprisoning its new king, Ferdinand VII, and installing on the Spanish throne his own brother, Joseph Bonaparte.

The shock of Napoleon's invasion was felt across the Spanish empire. In both Spain and Latin America, civilians who were loyal to the king organized themselves into groups to demonstrate their opposition to Napoleon. From 1808, unrest spread across Spain, prompted originally by Napoleon's deposition of the Spanish king Charles IV and then his heir, Ferdinand. In 1812, a constituent assembly at Cádiz proclaimed a liberal constitution in Spain. The proclamation had profound effects throughout the empire.

In South America, criollo revolutionaries took advantage of the confusion. They accused viceroys and other royal officials of disloyalty to the Spanish crown and organized "loyalist" demonstrations in major cities. In Caracas, Santiago, Bogotá, and Buenos Aires, local authorities surrendered to forces dominated by criollo loyalists.

True Spanish loyalists soon realized that the criollos were using loyalty as a smoke-screen for their real goal, independence. Inconclusive fighting broke out between loyalists and criollo patriots. The patriots failed to unite across the continent and remained largely uncoordinated. Independence became a chaotic scramble. Each region fought for what it could achieve.

The Great Liberators

The two inspired soldiers who emerged from the chaos to guide South America to freedom from Spain were Simón Bolívar and José de San Martín. Simón Bolívar (1783–1830) was born into one of the rich-

est and most powerful criollo landowning families of Venezuela. He was orphaned as a child, inherited a fortune, and received an education steeped in Enlightenment ideas.

As a young man, Bolívar traveled to Europe, where he fell in love with and married the daughter of a Spanish nobleman. The couple returned to Venezuela, where Bolívar's young bride died less than a year

This statue of Francisco de Miranda stands in Bogotá, Venezuela. Miranda was an early hero of Venezuelan independence but was later seen by many patriots as a traitor for his negotiations with the Spanish.

749

This map shows the locations of the major battles of the campaigns for independence in South America.

later. Devastated by her death, Bolívar returned to Europe, where he vowed to commemorate his wife's death by liberating Venezuela from Spanish rule.

José de San Martín (1778–1850) was born in 1778 in Argentina. Like Bolívar, he came from a wealthy criollo family. He was educated in Spain, where he fought with Spanish forces against Napoleon. In 1811, San Martín became a lieutenant colonel in the Spanish army. By this time, however, San Martín's goal was the liberation of his own country, and in 1812 he sailed for Buenos Aires.

Preparation for Independence

Bolívar's first involvement in the independence movement was as a follower of his compatriot Francisco de Miranda. In 1810, Miranda led patriots in a second revolt in Venezuela and briefly became dictator. In 1812, however, after a number of defeats and setbacks, Miranda tried to negotiate a peace with Spain that would allow him to escape. This appalled his colleagues, including Bolívar, who handed him over to the enemy. Miranda was deported to Cadíz, where he died in a dungeon in 1816.

Venezuela's independence movement was left without a leader. Bolívar assumed the role after he joined the Colombian army and defeated the Spanish at the Magdalena River. It was in this campaign that Bolívar's military genius became apparent. His strategy was to rely on swift movement and aggressive tactics. He judged soldiers on their individual merits rather than their social background or ethnic origins, so talented soldiers were able to progress. Bolívar's successes led to his promotion to general in the Colombian army; they also won him supporters for his developing plans for the liberation of Venezuela.

The Fight for Venezuela

Bolívar's army numbered only around 500 men. In a three-month march, Bolívar led his troops across jungles and swamps into Venezuela. In August 1813, Bolívar entered the capital, Caracas. Spanish troops withdrew from the city without a fight and Bolívar was welcomed as "the liberator."

This painting of Simón Bolívar's 1801 wedding hangs in his birthplace in Venezuela, now a museum dedicated to his life.

Bolívar's victory would be short lived. He offended his supporters by assuming the role of military dictator because he did not trust democracy. Bolívar failed to win over key sectors of society and lacked the support to transform his military victory into a more general one. When Napoleon lost power in Europe in 1814, Bolívar's position became even weaker.

With the Spanish king Ferdinand VII restored to the throne, royalist troops were sent to the Americas to fight the many independence movements breaking out there. In 1814, Spanish troops recaptured Caracas and Bolívar fled to Jamaica. By 1815 only Argentina was still in revolt; the Spanish had reconquered the rest of the continent.

Bolívar Makes New Plans

Undeterred, Bolívar remained dedicated to independence for his homeland and the rest of Latin America. In exile, he wrote his stirring *Letter from Jamaica*. This docu-ment confirmed Bolívar's dedication to the idea of a republic. He rejected the notion of monarchy as being foreign to the spirit of Latin America and asserted, "The bonds that united us to Spain have been severed."

Bolívar returned to Venezuela in 1817. This time, his guerrillas were accompanied

A likeness of Simón Bolívar appears on this box of Bolivar cigars from Havana, Cuba. Bolívar's achievements made him a hero throughout South America and the Caribbean.

This illustration from a book published in 1896 shows Bolívar's troops crossing a perilous mountain pass in 1819. The Spanish believed the mountains to be impassable and were taken by surprise by Bolívar's attack.

by British soldiers who found themselves out of work at the end of the Napoleonic Wars in Europe. This time, too, Bolívar was careful to ensure that all those who fought with him—including black slaves—were given political incentives to stay loyal. He also made an alliance with a guerrilla group of Indian plainsmen. The alliance was vital in broadening the ethnic basis of the revolution beyond the criollo population. It also gave Bolívar access to the central plains of Venezuela, allowing him to avoid the northern coastal area and Caracas, where Spanish troops waited for him. Bolívar set up a capital at Angostura and began planning to overthrow the Spanish viceroyalty of New Granada and its capital at Bogotá.

Crossing the Andes
Bolívar's attack on New Granada, including Colombia and Venezuela, was one of the most daring in military history. His strategy was a simple one of surprise. He would attack the Spanish from a totally unexpected direction. Bolívar advanced his army of only 2,500 men along rivers, across flooded plains, and then over the icy Colombian Andes. The soldiers endured terrible hardships in the freezing mountain passes.

The Spanish, who assumed that the Andes were impassable, were taken by surprise. Bolívar defeated them in a short battle at Boyacá in August 1819. Three days later, he entered Bogotá. The victory signaled the end of Spain's occupation of Colombia. Bolívar was named president of the new state of Gran Colombia, which at this stage included only part of Venezuela.

Expanding Gran Colombia
In 1821, Bolívar won the rest of Venezuela from Spain. He then turned his attention to the west, sending his outstanding lieutenant Antonio José de Sucre (1795–1830) to

invade Ecuador from the sea. Sucre and Bolívar advanced into the highlands and won a decisive victory over the Spanish at Pichincha in May 1822. Royalist resistance fell away, and Ecuador was incorporated into Bolívar's state of Gran Colombia.

Bolívar now controlled all the modern countries of Colombia, Ecuador, Panama, and Venezuela. He intended that Gran Colombia should form the beginnings of a federal republic similar to the United States. Bolívar also wanted to help liberate other parts of Latin America, such as Peru, so that they could join his great enterprise.

The Victories of San Martín

South America's other great liberator, José de San Martín, had been busy farther south. He had little to do in his homeland of Argentina, which had overthrown the Bourbon viceroy in 1810. Instead, San Martín turned to Chile, where a revolutionary called Bernardo O'Higgins had led a failed revolt between 1810 and 1814.

San Martín spent two years recruiting, training, and equipping his army. Training was essential because San Martín intended to lead his men on a perilous crossing of the Andes from Argentina into Chile. The arduous twenty-one day journey gave San Martín the vital element of surprise. In February 1817, he won a crucial battle that

This monument to Simón Bolívar was put up by admirers in Washington, D.C.

The cathedral dominates Plaza de Bolívar in Bogotá, Colombia. Bolívar's name is associated with squares, parks, and streets in many South American cities.

The Andes Mountains form an apparently impassable barrier but it was through these mountains that San Martín led his army to surprise the Spanish in Chile.

This nineteenth-century drawing shows casualties of the Battle of Ayacucho on December 9, 1824, in which José de Sucre defeated the Spanish in Peru.

left him in control of the Chilean capital, Santiago. The next year, a victory at Maipú proved decisive. Bernardo O'Higgins became the first independent ruler of Chile.

The Fall of Lima

With Chile liberated, San Martín turned to Peru, which he attacked from the sea. In 1820, he blockaded the capital, Lima, and captured the port of Pisco, about 100 miles (160 km) to the south. He delayed attacking the capital, hoping to gain its surrender.

In June 1821, the viceroy evacuated the city, withdrawing to the inland stronghold of Cuzco. The continued Spanish presence meant that Peruvian independence remained uncertain. It was not long before a large Spanish army emerged to take up position in front of Lima. San Martín did not have the men to overcome such odds, so he turned to Simón Bolívar for help.

Bolívar and Sucre in Peru

The two great liberators, San Martín and Bolívar, met for the first and only time in Guayaquil, Ecuador, on July 26, 1822. No one knows exactly what the two men discussed or what decisions they made. Most historians believe that San Martín probably asked Bolívar for help with the final push against the loyalists. Whatever happened at the meeting, San Martín left Peru shortly afterward, perhaps to allow Bolívar a free hand or perhaps because of his frustration with the situation.

Bolívar entered Peru in September 1823 and began amassing an army. Almost a year later, in August 1824, he and Antonio de Sucre defeated the Spanish at Junín. In

December 1824, Sucre alone won the decisive battle of Ayacucho. The victory signaled not only the start of Peruvian independence but the liberation of all South America from Spain.

Bolívar's dream of a United States of Gran Colombia was short lived. In 1830, both Venezuela and Ecuador seceded from the union; Bolívar resigned, sick and deeply disillusioned, and died the same year.

Brazil's Route to Independence

In contrast to Spanish South America, Portugal's only colony on the continent—Brazil—became an independent monarchy almost entirely without loss of life. Brazil in the eighteenth century was a poor, undeveloped country, yet one that was largely free of the ethnic tensions that were so strong elsewhere in South America. There were stirrings of patriotic zeal, however, especially after the American Revolutionary War. In 1788, the Portuguese crushed a revolutionary movement of intellectuals led by Joaquim José da Silva Xavier, a dentist-turned-soldier nicknamed Tiradentes, or "tooth puller."

In Portugal, as in Spain, Napoleon brought matters to a head. When Napoleon led his army into Portugal in 1807, the regent, Dom João, feared that he would be seized and imprisoned. With the help of the British navy, the entire Portuguese court and royal family fled to Brazil, arriving in January 1808. Rio de Janeiro immediately became the seat of the Portuguese royal family and the exiled capital of Portugal.

Dom João set about improving the poor, dirty city to make it fit for a king. He built a theater, created a press, and started industries with the help of British investors. Dom João became so enthusiastic about Brazil that he and his family stayed on after the defeat of Napoleon in 1815. Dom João granted Brazil equal status with Portugal, and in 1816, with the death of his mother, he became king of both countries.

A revolution in Portugal in 1820 finally forced Dom João to reassess the situation. Realizing that he was needed in Europe, he sailed from Brazil in 1821, leaving his son, Dom Pedro, as regent in Brazil.

The Emperor of Brazil

When it became obvious, in 1822, that Portugal was planning to reduce Brazil's status to that of a colony once again, the Brazilians were outraged. Many saw this as an opportunity to break from Portugal, and Dom Pedro agreed. Urged on by local

This monument at Guayaquil in Ecuador commemorates the only meeting between Bolívar and San Martín. No one knows what was said at the meeting. San Martín afterward went into exile, and some people suggest that he was disillusioned with Bolívar's response to his request for help.

This bust in Brasilia, Brazil, commemorates Tiradentes, the "tooth puller." The onetime dentist led an uprising against Portuguese rule in 1789; when it failed, he was executed.

By the late nineteenth century, when this photograph was taken, the influence of the former royal family had helped turn Rio de Janeiro into a modern, European-style city with broad avenues and imposing buildings.

patriots, Dom Pedro rejected his father's demand that he return to Europe. Instead, he publicly announced his intention to remain. By the end of 1822 he had been proclaimed Pedro I, emperor of Brazil.

Pedro's declaration of independence in Brazil was part of a process of continuity, not revolution. There was some resistance from Portuguese soldiers in Brazil, but they soon withdrew when faced with troops loyal to Pedro. Brazil's transition to independence was peaceful. The new country was, initially, well governed, as Pedro surrounded himself with capable advisers. In 1825, Pedro's father, Dom João, finally acknowledged Brazilian independence.

Abdication and Revolution

Pedro's popularity did not last. He waged a disastrous war on Argentina, which resulted in a huge loss of Brazilian territories. In 1831, he decided to abdicate in favor of his son, then only five years old, who became Pedro II.

Nine years later the young emperor took the full reins of power. He was to be an extremely popular ruler, overseeing the emergence of Brazil as a modern industrial state. Yet, by the 1880s, the very capitalists that Pedro himself helped to create regarded the monarchy as obsolete. As popular discontent grew, the army stepped in to depose the emperor in 1889. Brazil had become a republic.

South America After Independence

The Years of the Political Strongmen

After the countries of South America won their independence from Spain and Portugal in the early nineteenth century (*see 6:747*), much of the region fell into chaos. The dreams of political unity that inspired the independence movement in Spanish-speaking South America crumbled. Some people blame this fracturing on the divisive effect of the continent's towering mountains and huge plains. The success of Portuguese-speaking Brazil in maintaining political unity over a vast area despite geographical extremes, however, suggests that politics rather than geography were the key factor in the disintegration of other countries.

Political Tensions and Divisions
There were several reasons for the lack of unity in Spain's former colonies. Although they had secured independence, the new states still operated within social and political structures that had been put in place under Spanish rule. The region remained burdened by its colonial past. When the United States had become independent in 1781, by contrast, it took immediate steps to abandon its colonial heritage and create its own institutions (*see 4:561*).

The class that had long seen itself as legitimate rulers in the region was the criollo elite, born in South America of European descent. Although criollos led the struggle for independence, few gave much thought to the practicalities of ruling once the colonial authorities had left. More important, the criollo elite in each country was bitterly divided between liberal and conservative factions. How could the criollos bring unity to South America when they were unable to agree among themselves?

Coffee trees cover hillsides in modern-day Brazil. The country became the world's largest exporter of coffee during the economic expansion of the second half of the nineteenth century.

757

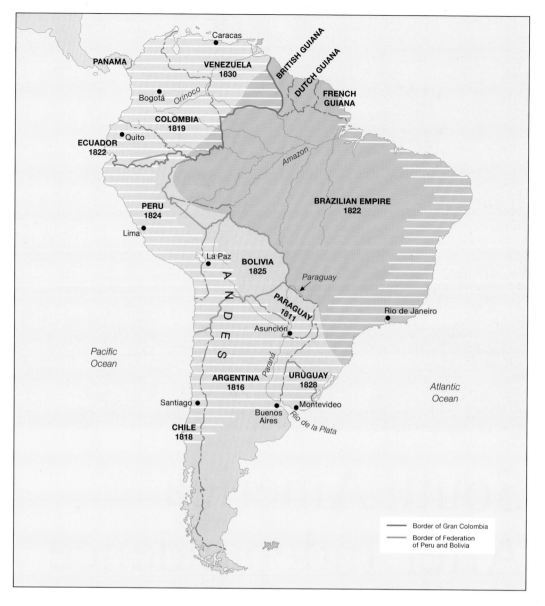

This map shows the political divisions of South America as nations emerged after liberation. The area hatched with white lines shows the parts of the continent that had previously been under the effective control of Spain and Portugal.

The divisions within the ruling elite were exacerbated by lack of money. The long wars of independence left each of the new countries virtually bankrupt. Weak government and economic problems created a climate in which political power was liable to be won by caudillos, strong, charismatic leaders, often from military backgrounds.

Bolívar's Attempted Union

Throughout the campaign for independence, the great military leader Simón Bolívar dreamed of creating a union of Latin American countries, rather like the United States of America. In 1823, most of the countries of Central America formed their own federation. In 1826, as ruler of the new state of Gran Colombia—comprising what are now Colombia, Venezuela, Ecuador, and Panama—Bolívar sought to implement his scheme. He wanted to form an alliance with Peru and Bolivia but the other two countries were unenthusiastic. Worse, Gran Colombia itself began to fall apart as Venezuela and Ecuador refused to be ruled from Bogotá in Colombia.

Disillusioned, Bolívar left the continent he had done so much to liberate and went into self-imposed exile in Europe. Shortly before he died in 1830, he made a bitter prediction for South America's future: "[South] America is ungovernable. Those who have served the revolution have plowed the sea."

Constant political instability seemed to justify Bolívar's pessimism. Countries were split by different cultures and by different classes. Urban workers felt they had no stake in the new governments, while large rural Indian populations wanted little to do with European-dominated urban centers, even if it meant losing their rights as citizens. The continent was also home to African slaves—in 1888, Brazil became the last South American country to ban slavery—while mestizos, a huge group of mixed Spanish and Indian descent, had their own agenda and aims.

The mestizos were frustrated by their lack of political power, and they distrusted the criollo ruling class. Yet the criollos themselves faced competition from the Catholic Church and landowners, who also wanted the political system to promote their particular interests. There was little chance of unity among the rival groups.

The Politics of Violence

Between 1825 and 1850, violence became an accepted part of politics in South America. Landowners first began to use private armies to protect themselves and their land. Troops with fighting experience from the wars of independence were used to settle local political disputes. Finally, military strength allowed strongmen to seize power at a national level. Virtually every country in Spanish-speaking South America—Chile was the only exception—fell under the cult of the caudillo.

In power, caudillos tended to remain true to the self-ambition that got them there. They were rarely interested in changing political or economic structures to benefit the country: many were staunch supporters of the social order, the Catholic Church, and traditional economics. Caudillos concentrated on holding on to power.

The basis of a caudillo's support was personal charisma, so that this type of politics was sometimes called *personalismo*.

The most important element in a caudillo's personality was manliness, which was acknowledged in the Spanish compliment "muy hombre," which literally means "very man." The caudillo's reliance on his personality meant that he had little chance of passing his power on to a successor.

Caudillos came from every social class. Whatever their origins, however, they were treated like monarchs once in power. South

An overseer supervises African slaves making sugar in Brazil around 1850. Brazil, which did not abolish slavery until 1888, has a high proportion of citizens of African descent.

This engraving, made during his lifetime, shows the Argentinian caudillo Juan Manuel Rosas, who led the country for nearly two decades and waged a brutal war against the Indians of the pampas.

759

This ornate silver belt buckle was made during the nineteenth century for a gaucho, a cowboy from Argentina. Gauchos often wore ostentatious buckles, spurs, saddles, and other pieces of equipment.

American society traditionally looked up to a king as the head of the social order. The caudillo simply took the king's place.

The culture of the caudillo—caudillismo—was at its strongest immediately after independence. In Central America, the Federation of Central American Republics set up in 1823 collapsed. Warlords ruled Colombia, Peru, Ecuador, and Uruguay. Paraguay and Venezuela were led by paternalistic dictatorships that suffered frequent military coups.

Even Brazil, which was ruled by Emperor Pedro II, suffered a decade of civil unrest after 1835 when a group of caudillos led a number of rebellions aimed at overthrowing the monarchy and decentralizing the country. The government defeated the uprisings with the help of the country's poorest citizens, black Brazilians and native Indians, who feared the arrogance of the caudillos.

Scarlet Ribbons

In Argentina, the caudillo Juan Manuel Rosas (1793–1877) abused his authority to exile those who opposed his rule and to demand public demonstrations of loyalty. A wealthy landowner and cattle rancher, Rosas had built up an army of gauchos, Argentina's notoriously wild, lawless cowboys. In 1829, he used his army to seize the governorship of Buenos Aires, which he ruled until 1832, when he set off on a bloody campaign against the Indians.

In 1835, Rosas became governor again, this time extending his authority over most of Argentina, using espionage, intimidation,

In this nineteenth-century engraving, a gaucho pursues a running bird called a rhea. The gaucho is about to throw his bola, a weighted rope that will wrap itself around the bird's legs.

and even murder to suppress any signs of opposition. Rosas made citizens of Buenos Aires wear a red ribbon as a sign of loyalty. Even aristocratic ladies dared not walk the streets without a red ribbon sash. Rosas's wife, Doña Encarnación, wore scarlet satin evening dresses and ranchers wore scarlet ponchos.

Most liberals and intellectuals fled Argentina, leaving Rosas's position even stronger. He ruled as a dictator for seventeen years. Only when he led a military campaign in 1852 in support of an ousted caudillo from neighboring Uruguay was Rosas finally overthrown by a combination of foreign troops and Argentinian rebels.

The Stability of Chile
Unlike its neighbors, Chile avoided being taken over by a caudillo. After independence, Chile first turned to its revolutionary leader Bernardo O'Higgins, who governed until he was forced to resign in 1823. Chile was then governed by a series of liberal dictatorships.

In 1830, a powerful group of landowners and merchants, supported by the army, took control with the aim of creating a stronger government. In 1833, they passed a new constitution giving sovereignty to a centralized, governing body while at the same time allowing the army and the Catholic Church to retain many of their traditional powers. The 1833 constitution laid the basis for a long period of stability and economic growth.

Chilean stability probably owed as much to the country's geography as to its political system. The long, narrow shape of the country made it susceptible to domination by a small, close-knit group of landowners. The country had relatively few of the ethnic divisions that split other South American regions: there were few Indian communities, and the black slave population was declining.

Land Ownership and Peonage
Elsewhere in South America, violence and caudillismo added to the continent's economic difficulties. The crucial problem, however, had its roots in the colonial era: land ownership. After independence, most of the new republics had distributed land among their supporters to ensure loyalty and as a form of political reward. Landowners then rented out their properties to small farmers, many of whom were already living on the land. These small farmers could not afford to pay their new landlords, so they were forced into debt, on which the landowners charged high rates of interest.

The republican governments made the farmers' position worse by taxing agricultural produce rather than the land on which it grew. This policy burdened the small farmers, who actually grew the produce, with paying taxes rather than the landowning elite. The farmers were forced even further into debt, giving rise to a system unique to Latin America: peonage.

Peonage tied a laborer to working for a landlord in order to pay off his debt, but while he worked the debt kept increasing. When a peon died, his son would inherit his debt, so laborers' families had no hope

Two workers carry bananas along a country road in the Central American country of Honduras. The dependence of Honduras and neighboring Nicaragua on bananas earned them the nickname "banana republics," which today is still sometimes used as a dismissive reference to any small tropical state.

An Araucanian Indian woman from Chile weaves while her baby sleeps in a carrying frame in this photograph from the middle of the nineteenth century. Preserving traditional practices and remaining outside the urbanized European culture, the Indians were excluded from Latin America's growing prosperity.

of escape from indebtedness. The peonage system was partly responsible for inhibiting the emergence of a middle class in Latin America.

The Church Opts Out

The one possible source of help for the indebted poor was the Catholic Church. Instead, however, the deeply conservative church chose to support the ruling elite and the caudillos. In any case, the church's position in Latin America had been weakened by the Vatican's reluctance to recognize the republics after independence. The church had wanted to see Iberia retain control of its colonies. Congregations shrank, fewer new priests joined, and the church lost its moral authority, a loss that added to the general lawlessness of the region up to 1850.

Time for Change

From about the middle of the nineteenth century, the South American republics began to change. There were many reasons for this. Among them was the growing realization that politics alone could not provide a solution to the continent's end-

less cycles of upheaval and unrest. As early as the 1840s in Chile and the 1850s and 1860s in Argentina and Brazil, people in positions of authority started to realize that the previous approaches had failed and looked elsewhere for answers.

A new group of progressive leaders, the "generation of the forties and fifties," had grown up in postindependent Latin America and had never lived under a monarchy. These liberal thinkers wanted to modernize their countries through a combination of economic expansion and political stability. They saw Great Britain and the United States as models of successful democratic governments, recognizing how closely those countries' achievements were related to economic progress.

The South American republics became obsessed with economic advancement, which dominated the continent from 1850 to 1914 as completely as caudillismo had dominated the previous period. At the same time, the Catholic Church set out to regain the influence it had lost. It reformed its clergy, who once more began working among the poor, particularly in rural areas.

In 1850, there was little industry in Latin America. Beyond a limited amount of mining, the republics' economies were agricultural. Economic expansion could only come through increased mineral production and raising livestock, cereals, coffee, and bananas for the export market. Brazil, Argentina, and Uruguay made their agriculture more commercial, and cattle ranching grew into a complex, modern business. Brazil soon became the world's largest exporter of coffee and raw rubber. In Central America, bananas became the sole export crop of Nicaragua and Honduras, earning them the enduring nickname of "banana republics."

By growing produce specifically for export markets, Latin America made itself economically dependent on Europe and the United States. Both continents invested heavily in the region, particularly in Brazil, which was considered politically stable under Pedro II (1825–1891). Argentina, Chile, and Mexico also offered investment opportunities as their governments grew more stable. By 1914, British investments in Argentina were so high that the country was referred to as an economic colony of Britain. Latin American countries with a high percentage of Indians, such as Peru and Colombia, were still regarded as inherently unstable and received much less foreign investment.

Growing Territorial Ambitions

As South America grew increasingly wealthy, the ownership of potentially valuable land became a source of national conflict, especially as boundaries had not always been drawn accurately after independence. Chile had already been to war against Peru and Bolivia in 1836 to prevent their forming a commercial confederation. In the 1870s, a sharp decline in demand struck the copper exports on which Chile depended, causing a recession and political instability. Chile solved the problem by increasing nitrate production from land it controlled in Peruvian and Bolivian territory. Increased demand for nitrates—an important material in the emerging chemical industries (*see 6:794*)—provoked a dis-

A ruined office marks the site of a nineteenth-century mine in the Atacama Desert in Chile. The desert was the world's largest source of sodium nitrate, which was in great demand in the nineteenth century for making fertilizers and explosives.

This engraving from 1866 shows Brazilian troops in a trench during the Paraguayan War, or War of the Triple Alliance (1865–1870), a territorial conflict in which Brazil, Argentina, and Uruguay allied to resist expansion by Paraguay.

pute over the ownership of the nitrate fields. The dispute led to the War of the Pacific (1879–1883), from which Chile emerged victorious.

On the opposite side of the continent, Argentina also went to war to expand its territories. Victory in the Paraguayan War, or War of the Triple Alliance (1865–1870), brought new lands in the north and northwest. The Desert Campaign of 1879 to 1880 added vast areas for cultivation and settlement in the south. This expansion, however, only came at the cost of virtually exterminating the nomadic Indians who lived on the pampas, or plains. Argentina's military successes aided its rapid economic growth, which stood at 5 percent per year. By the outbreak of World War I, Argentina was one of the richest nations in the world.

The increased export market to Europe and North America required modern infrastructures. Railroads spread, mainly in Argentina, but also in Mexico, Chile, and Brazil. Steel bridges were built and telegraph lines laid. The first modern water and sewerage systems appeared in the 1850s, and telephone systems were introduced in the 1880s.

Increased economic growth permitted prosperous urban upper and middle classes to display their new wealth by building impressive apartments and villas in cities such as Buenos Aires, Rio de Janeiro, São Paulo, Lima, Mexico City, and Caracas. The rich were accustomed to travel to Europe for opera and other cultural activities, but now many South American cities could build their own magnificent opera houses, zoos, and botanical gardens.

The Indians

At the bottom of the social scale, the Indians were virtually excluded from economic progress. Working hard in the countryside, using traditional tools and techniques, they enjoyed little improvement in their standard of living. They continued to live in peonage and were treated as an inferior race by people of European descent.

European dominance grew throughout the century as Latin American countries encouraged immigration from Europe to boost the population and improve economic progress. The European elite did not consider the Indians to be part of the economic boom. They also saw the Catholic Church as an obstacle to progress. In Chile, Venezuela, El Salvador, and Mexico, strict laws were passed to separate the church from the state and to bring the church under government control.

American and British flags fly at the official opening of a bridge on Peru's Central Railroad in the later nineteenth century. Americans had built the railroad, which the British owned.

Into the Twentieth Century

By the start of the twentieth century, the Latin American republics—Brazil ceased to be a monarchy in 1889—had stopped fighting among themselves. In 1907, these republics were invited to the Hague Peace Conference in Europe, which tried to avoid the looming prospect of war. It was the first time that Latin America contributed to such a worldwide meeting.

At the same time, Latin American countries were becoming more aware that the biggest threat to their safety came from the ambitions of the United States. The United

An overseer from Barbados poses with Amazon Indians at a rubber plantation in Brazil during the 1890s. European and American demand for automobile and bicycle tires helped create a boom in the rubber industry. Despite having abolished African slavery in 1888, the Brazilians effectively enslaved the native inhabitants of the Amazon to collect raw rubber.

765

This village in the coastal highlands of Venezuela reflects the traditional national architecture of the German immigrants who founded the village in 1842. Throughout the nineteenth century, Latin America was one of the favorite destinations for European emigrants.

States controlled Cuba, having won the island's freedom from Spain in the Spanish-American War of 1898 (*see 6:835*). The United States also interfered to ensure that Panama won its independence from neighboring Colombia in 1903. When the Panama Canal opened in 1914, the United States had a virtual stranglehold over the Panamanian economy.

Under President Theodore Roosevelt, the United States exercised the right put forth in the Monroe Doctrine of 1823 to interfere anywhere on the American continents. With Roosevelt's "big stick" policy, the United States appointed itself the hemispheric police power enjoying privileges in other countries' affairs.

The problem with the policy was that the United States became not only the region's police but also its judge. Intervention relied not on moral or humanitarian concerns but on U.S. financial interests. The big stick was felt mainly in Central America and the Caribbean, where the United States overthrew governments and created puppet dictatorships sympathetic toward U.S. businesses. By 1914, the United States supplied Latin America with a third of its imports and purchased over a third of all the region's exports.

The Effects of World War I

When World War I broke out in Europe in 1914, Latin American reaction reflected the region's suspicion of the United States. Although the region's ruling elite had great sympathy for France, only eight nations joined the Allies in declaring war on Germany, while Brazil and Cuba alone offered military aid to the Allies. Chile, Argentina, Colombia, and Mexico remained neutral.

The outbreak of war brought a virtual halt to Latin America's international trade. By the end of the war, however, the demands of war-torn Europe supported an industrial boom in exported food and strategic materials. Prosperity also grew with the development of industries to manufacture goods for the home market that could no longer be obtained from Europe.

The conflict appeared to have left Latin America prosperous and stable. The appearance was an illusion, however. The nations remained fragile, weakened by deep racial divisions that diminished any sense of united nationhood. Economies reliant on the export market remained vulnerable to external influences. In the uncertain future, Latin America would turn to a familiar solution: the caudillo (*see 7:976*).

China in the Nineteenth Century

Western Threats to the Heavenly Kingdom

In September 1793, Ch'ien-lung, emperor of China, learned that "barbarians" from the West had arrived at the port of Macao. Bearing gifts, they had come to wish the emperor well on his birthday. The visitors were, in fact, a delegation from Great Britain led by Lord Macartney, who hoped to persuade China to open its ports to free trade with the British and to grant them diplomatic representation. Macartney fared no better than earlier ambassadors from what the emperor called "the lonely remoteness of your island, cut off from the world by intervening wastes of sea."

Ch'ien-lung explained that China had no need of foreign trade. He accepted Macartney's presents in the same way as he would tribute from China's satellite states and sent a polite message thanking King George III for his "submissive loyalty."

For his part, Macartney broke Chinese etiquette by refusing to perform the traditional kowtow before the emperor. The kowtow involved going down on both knees and knocking one's forehead on the floor in a gesture of submission. Macartney simply knelt on one knee, as he would before the British monarch.

A tattered photograph from the late nineteenth century shows Chinese traders and a barber in the street. The development of business was hampered by the lack of investment in facilities such as shops.

767

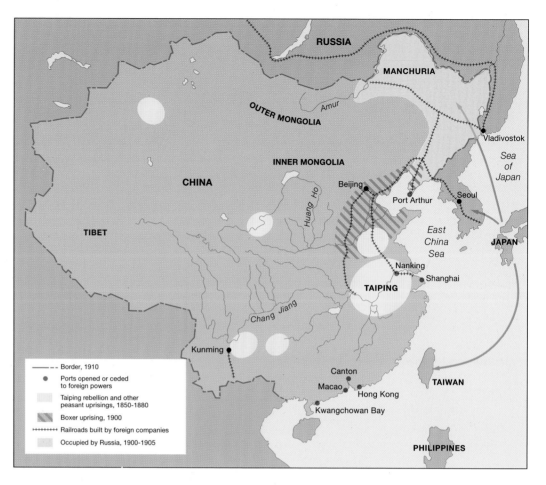

This map shows China in the nineteenth century. The Ching dynasty faced challenges from internal rebellion, the encroachment of European trade, and aggression from Russia and Japan.

Chinese Culture

The meeting between the representatives of two of the world's leading powers was symbolic of the gulf that existed between West and East. China had been isolated for centuries, secure in the knowledge that it was the center of the world, its emperor owed tribute from all other nations (*see 4:523*). Indifferent to the outside world, the empire was also, in its internal government and social structure, proof against change. Dynasties might rise and fall, famines come and go, peasant insurrections rage or be quelled. The country's government was still based on the eternal truths that had been laid out by the philosopher Confucius in the fifth century B.C.E.

China's attitude made economic sense. Virtually self-sufficient in food, it had little need for the manufactured goods Europe had to offer. Trade with the West had gone on for about three centuries, chiefly with England, but remained limited to a simple triangular exchange. English textiles were exported to India, Indian cotton to China, and Chinese tea, silk, and porcelain to England (*see 4:532*).

The Chinese controlled trade with the West tightly. Since 1757, European traders had been limited to a single port, Canton. By 1800, no more than a thousand Europeans dealt with the bribe-seeking guild of merchants, the Cohong, which officials of the Manchu, or Ching, dynasty established to operate an effective government monopoly on trade.

Signs of Change

Macartney's reception was evidence that the Chinese view of the world had not altered, despite centuries of contact with other parts of the globe. A few years earlier, however, a small event had occurred that held great portent for the future. Since the sixteenth century, Jesuit missionaries had served at the emperor's court, where to gain acceptance they were forced to graft Chinese beliefs such as ancestor worship onto Christian teaching (*see 4:528*). In the early eighteenth century, the pope banned such an adulteration of Christian truths.

Too obscure to be seen at the time, the incident's message was that, unlike previous barbarians, Europeans would not easily be assimilated by Chinese culture. China faced an economically aggressive and technologically advanced challenger. It was ill equipped to resist.

China's Problems

The previous barbarians assimilated by China included the ruling Manchu Chinese themselves. Originating from the region of Manchuria in the north, the Manchu

A rice-paper painting from the mid–nineteenth century shows a Chinese woman smoking opium. Smokers used long pipes to allow the smoke to cool down enough to inhale.

had invaded China in the 1640s to establish their own Ching dynasty, based in Beijing. After more than a century of Manchu rule, China found itself facing a number of difficulties. Peasant resentment of the foreign rulers nourished abundant secret societies and cults throughout the country. To that resentment was added mounting economic hardship. Between 1750 and 1850, China's population nearly doubled, from something over 200 million to 430 million, creating a land shortage. At the same time, China's peasants suffered from inflation in the price of silver, which was used to pay taxes.

The Opium Trade

From midcentury, silver inflation was increasingly caused by the British. Britain's triangular trade with India and China had a flaw: the value of the goods sold to China was lower than the cost of those imported back to Britain. The British covered the deficiency with supplementary payments of silver until, in the 1830s, they found a way to make the China trade more profitable.

Millions of Chinese were addicted to smoking opium, a drug produced from the seeds of a variety of poppy that induced a deep reverie. India, meanwhile, had an unlimited supply of the opium poppy.

Printed on silk in the nineteenth century, this image depicts Chinese laborers working in a paddy field. To support China's growing population, more and more marginal land, or land that was difficult to farm, was turned over to agriculture.

Although opium was illegal in China, foreign merchants found it easy to use bribery to smuggle it past customs officials on a large scale. Between 1760 and 1840, China's imports of opium soared from only 1,000 chests a year to 40,000. Britain's silver payments to China fell as the profits from the opium trade rose, causing silver inflation in China.

The Opium Wars

The Ching authorities determined to end the opium trade. The fateful decision revealed the dynasty's inability to defend itself and ushered in a series of humiliations that would eventually spell the doom of imperial China.

In 1839, China ordered foreign, chiefly British, merchants to hand over their stocks of opium and stop trafficking in the drug. A few days later, tension boiled over into war when some drunken British sailors killed a Chinese villager. In the Opium War (1839–1842), Chinese forces crumpled in an unequal fight against the British navy.

The 1842 Treaty of Nanking that ended the war was a bitter blow to Chinese self-esteem. China agreed to pay £21 million to compensate for confiscated opium and war indemnities, to open five ports to British trade, and to cede the port of Hong Kong to Great Britain. The treaty did not mention the opium trade, implicitly acknowledging China's inability to stop it.

In the next two decades, other nations followed where Great Britain had led. The United States, by a treaty of 1844, gained the same rights as the British and consular jurisdiction over Americans in China. That same year, France gained favored-nation status and the right to erect Roman Catholic churches in the treaty ports. China was already a prime area of activity for Christian missionaries, who found a ready supply of converts, mainly among urban China's poor. This Christian penetration of China contributed to the outbreak of the Taiping Rebellion in the 1850s.

In 1856, French and British troops fought another Opium War. After four years of fighting and the foreign occupation of Beijing, the Chinese legalized the importation of opium.

The Taiping Rebellion

The instability of the Ching regime and Christian activity in China formed the backdrop to the greatest of the many peasant insurrections in Chinese history, the Taiping Rebellion of the 1850s and 1860s. The rebellion was led by Hung Hsiu-ch'uan, a village schoolteacher from a peasant background. Declaring himself to be a younger brother of Christ, Hung developed a revolutionary creed that mixed Christianity and classical Chinese tradition. His mission was to overthrow the Ching dynasty and establish a Heavenly Kingdom of Peace: *Taiping* means "heavenly kingdom." He gathered an armed following in the southern province of Guangxi, attracted by the goal of an egalitarian society in which all property was to be held in common and in which women would share social and educational equality with men. By coincidence, Hung developed his creed at the very time that Karl Marx and Friedrich Engels were publishing the similarly utopian *Communist Manifesto* in Europe (*see 6:812*).

Western Interference

In 1850, Hung proclaimed himself emperor of the Kingdom of Peace and went to war against the Ching. He captured Nanking in 1853 and established the Taiping capital there, beyond the reach of Beijing. This time Western powers came to the aid of the

A detail from Beijing's Monument to the People's Heroes, built in 1958, celebrates the Taiping Rebellion against the foreign Ching dynasty.

Made in the nineteenth century, these delicate carved jade disks are fine examples of an art form the Chinese call *Bi,* or *Pi.*

Ching rulers. Although at first tolerant of the rebellion's mix of Chinese tradition and Christianity, Europeans quickly became alarmed by Hung's denunciations of trading concessions to the foreigners. In 1860, British and French troops fought the rebels at Shanghai, which had become the largest port for foreign trade. European firepower won the day.

When Hung died in 1864, the rebellion was already a spent force. Sporadic uprisings continued to break out, however. By the time the last was crushed in 1878, more than 30 million lives had been lost—more people than would die in World War I—and vast areas of China lay depopulated.

The Aftermath of Rebellion
The Taiping Rebellion exposed the military backwardness of the Ching armies and showed that Chinese culture was vulnerable to an ideology that drew on Western sources. The only imaginable obstacle to further Western penetration, a vigorous Taiping state, had been removed. The Europeans were quick to take advantage. In 1864, Russia had taken possession of the western corner of Xinjiang, having already won Chinese territory in the Amur Valley north of Korea (*see 5:696*).

The Taiping Rebellion also greatly increased the local authority of the warlords

who helped put it down. Their military and financial independence signaled a process of decentralization that gathered pace and would eventually contribute to the collapse of the empire. The Ching court, meanwhile, despite ruling over a discontented people and facing expansionist European powers superior in arms, technology, and wealth, refused to concede that reform was imperative. The Ching aristocracy and its Chinese officials were reluctant to contemplate innovations. Left to themselves, they would have maintained China's economic and social structure intact.

Westernizing China
A small group of highly placed officials, who came to be known as the Westerners, did manage to effect some changes in the name of strengthening China. They introduced Western manufacturing methods for arms production, most famously at the Kiangnan arsenal at Shanghai in 1865. In 1878, a modern coal mine opened in K'aip'ing. The first telegraph line and textile factories followed in the 1880s.

As the century wore on, events lent urgency to the Westerners' calls for reform. The European powers, racing to build colonial empires, inflicted on China a succession of territorial losses. In the 1880s, France absorbed most of Indochina, the peninsula between China and India over whose northern regions the Chinese traditionally exerted great influence. Meanwhile, Britain annexed Burma, and Portugal took outright possession of Macao.

The Sino-Japanese War
The biggest shock to China came at the hands of a neighbor, Japan, in the Sino-Japanese war of 1894 and 1895. Japan had unilaterally recognized the independence of Korea, for centuries a vassal state of China, in 1876. When a revolt broke out there in 1894, the Japanese tried to secure that independence by force. As Chinese troops went to the aid of the Korean king, Japan declared war on China and easily occupied Manchuria, Taiwan, and the Liaotung Peninsula. China was forced to submit to the harsh Treaty of Shimonoseki in 1895.

The treaty gave Taiwan and the Liaotung Peninsula to Japan and compelled China to relinquish power over Korea and pay a huge war indemnity. Within six days, Germany, France, and Russia, fearful of Japanese power, forced Japan to hand back the peninsula. Its return only underlined how deeply in debt China was to the Western powers. To pay the war indemnity required loans from Western governments.

This engraving shows Chinese workers putting finishing touches to a modern gunboat in 1883. China's first shipyard on Western lines opened in 1866, with European machinery and managers.

Japan, meanwhile, gained trading concessions in China as a most favored nation on a par with the West.

Defeat at the hands of a people on whom the Chinese traditionally looked down brought the debate about China's future into the open. The imperial court could no longer ignore the warnings of the reformers. A stream of edicts was announced by Emperor Kuang-hsü in 1898 in what became known as the Hundred Days of Reform. Whether they might have saved the dynasty is uncertain. As soon as they were issued, they were withdrawn, victims of a power struggle between the emperor and the dowager empress, Tzu-hsi.

Tzu-hsi, widow of the previous emperor, seized control of the government, locked up the emperor, and, in a last flourish of reaction, lent her weight to a rising wave of

Inhabitants of Shanghai watch the launch of the first train service in China in the summer of 1876.

773

The Boxer Rebellion

With the government unable to resist European advances into China, resistance fell instead to a secret society called Righteous and Harmonious Fists. Europeans dubbed society members Boxers, because one of their ritual dances used boxing movements. Adherents believed that such rituals made them superhuman and unable to be harmed by bullets.

The Boxers emerged in northern China in the second half of the nineteenth century, with the primary aim of destroying the Ching dynasty. They were also opposed to the foreigners who enjoyed privileged lifestyles in China. When the Chinese government became more conservative in 1898, it encouraged the Boxers to join with the dynasty in opposing the foreigners. Boxers enrolled in local militia groups.

What particularly provoked the Boxers were the practices of Christian missionaries in China. Chinese who converted to Christianity, who were mainly from the lower classes, abandoned traditional Chinese customs and ceremonies. The Boxers believed that they also received favorable treatment in legal disputes, thanks to European backing.

In 1899, the Boxers began attacking Chinese Christians and Western missionaries. The following summer, gangs of Boxers were roaming the countryside around Beijing. Alarmed, European governments combined to send a relief force of around 2,000 troops to protect foreigners in the capital. Tzu-hsi ordered imperial troops to bar their way from the northern coast to Beijing.

Inside the capital, meanwhile, the Boxer revolt had flowered into full-scale rebellion. Boxers burned churches and the homes of foreigners and killed Chinese they suspected of being Christians. When European powers seized coastal forts to enable another advance on Beijing, Tzu-

American troops in the campaign to relieve the siege of Beijing raise the Stars and Stripes above the city's Tartar Wall in this contemporary illustration.

A Western minister and his family walk past U.S. infantrymen lining a road in Beijing's Forbidden City after the city fell to a combined Western and Japanese force during the Boxer Rebellion.

Captured by U.S. cavalry, Boxer rebels await their fate in this photograph taken around 1901. The Western powers imposed heavy fines on China as punishment for the incident.

hsi ordered that all foreigners be killed. The German minister in Beijing was murdered. All the other members of the foreign legations, together with their families and Chinese servants, were besieged in their quarters or in the Roman Catholic cathedral. The 533 defenders resisted the Boxers, who were aided by government troops, for two months.

Meanwhile, imperial governors in some parts of China refused to obey Tzu-hsi's orders, instead suppressing Boxers in their territory. After the rebellion ended, the Chinese government used the fact as a basis to argue that the rebellion did not actually have official backing but was purely a peasant uprising in the northeast of the country.

In August 1900, an international relief force finally managed to fight its way into Beijing. The troops began a terrible sack of the city, looting anything of value. Tzu-hsi and most of the imperial court, meanwhile, fled to take refuge in Xi'an. A year later, a treaty ordered the Chinese to pay reparations to the foreign governments affected by the uprising.

The dowager empress Tzu-hsi in a photograph taken around 1904. Tzu-hsi rose from being a low-ranking concubine to become the most powerful individual in China.

antiforeign sentiment in China, represented by the revival of a cult known to Europeans as the Boxers (*see 6:774*). Foreign troops entered Beijing in 1900 to suppress a Boxer uprising.

The Boxer Rebellion proved costly for China. The dowager empress fled, while the Chinese granted further concessions to foreigners. Just as attempts at reform had come to nought in 1898, now conservative reaction had failed to protect China from overseas predators. Elements of Chinese society—army officers, students, intellectuals, Chinese abroad, and Westerners in government service—began to wonder whether the only solution was revolution.

Resisting Revolution

The Ching made one last attempt to stave off revolution by reform. A parliamentary constitution emerged between 1905 and 1908, but it was little more than a mask to cover the perpetuation of autocracy. The momentum in Chinese domestic affairs passed to a group of young men who in 1905 formed a revolutionary cabal called the Society of Sworn Confederates.

The leader of the society was a medical doctor called Sun Yat-sen. His message was that the woes of the country were not the work of the foreigners but of the Manchu and their blinkered devotion to China's ancient ways. The society's program was enshrined in three People's Principles. By the principle of nationality, the rule of the Manchu was to be overthrown; by the principle of the people's authority, or democracy, a constitutional republic was to replace the empire; and by the principle of the people's livelihood, a socialist redistribution of land would be pursued, along with a more general social policy to avert the injustices and inequalities of capitalism.

End of the Empire

In 1907, Kuang-hsü and Tzu-hsi died within four weeks of each other. The dowager empress had probably ordered the emperor poisoned from her deathbed. His successor agreed to reform the administration and govern by a cabinet, but when the names of its members were released in May 1911, eight of them turned out to be Manchu.

A few months later, China's long imperial history reached its close. The government provoked revolt in Szechwan by announcing its intention to take central control of all future railroad building. It intended to bypass the associations of Chinese merchants and gentry who wished to build railways with their own capital, instead relying on loans from abroad for construction. The announcement provoked revolt throughout the Chang Valley. The Society of Sworn Confederates attached itself to the uprising. By December, all but four provinces had come out against the Ching dynasty. Nanking was captured in December, and a provisional government established under the leadership of Yuan Shih-k'ai, an officer in the imperial army who had taken command of the rebel forces.

On December 25, Sun Yat-sen returned from a visit to the United States. Four days later, by a vote of representatives of the provisional governments established in the provinces, he was elected the first president of the Chinese republic. In honor of a previous agreement, however, he yielded his place to Yuan. When the last Manchu emperor formally abdicated in February 1912, China began its republican experiment under military rule (*see 7:933*).

Nineteenth-Century Japan

The Rise of an Asian Giant

In the nineteenth century Japan emerged from an isolated, feudal society to become a major player on the world stage, both militarily and economically. More remarkably still, the greatest change took place in a little over three decades, starting in 1868. The origin of this huge leap forward was an aristocratic revolution that deposed the country's military dictator and restored power to the emperor.

The Tokugawa Shogunate

At the beginning of the nineteenth century, Japan was firmly under the control of a feudal military ruler known as the shogun. There was also an emperor and an imperial court, but since the twelfth century, real power had been wielded by the shogun, who was officially the emperor's military deputy. Like the emperor's, the shogun's position was hereditary, and since 1603 it had been held by members of the same

family, the Tokugawa (*see 4:533*). The period during which they controlled Japan is known as the Tokugawa shogunate.

To demonstrate his independence from the emperor, the first Tokugawa shogun moved the capital from Kyoto, the ancient seat of the emperors, to Edo, now known as Tokyo. He and his successors further asserted their power by subduing Japan's great class of landowning princes, the daimyo, together with their retainers, the aristocratic sword-bearing warriors called samurai. The Tokugawa shoguns imposed a hostage system that forced the daimyo to spend part of the year on their estates and part at Edo. Whenever they left the capital, the daimyo had to leave behind their wives and families as pledges of their loyalty and good behavior.

Such strict controls created resentment. The need to maintain two homes was a major financial drain for the daimyo, as

This woodblock print of Japan's Mount Fuji was created by the renowned artist Katsushika Hokusai (1760–1849). Hokusai created a whole series of images featuring the mountain, a national symbol of Japan.

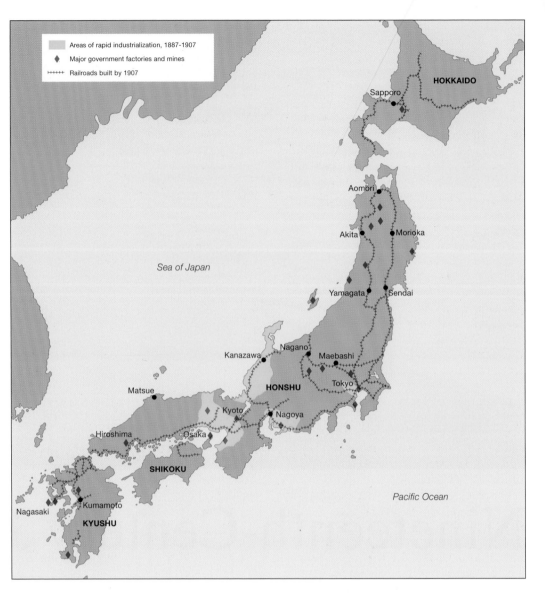

Areas of rapid industrialization, 1887-1907

◆ Major government factories and mines

+++++ Railroads built by 1907

HOKKAIDO

Sapporo

Aomori

Akita
Morioka

Sea of Japan

Yamagata
Sendai

Kanazawa
Nagano
Maebashi

Matsue
HONSHU
Tokyo

Kyoto
Nagoya

Hiroshima
Osaka

Pacific Ocean

SHIKOKU

Nagasaki
Kumamoto

KYUSHU

This map of Japan in the nineteenth century shows the country's major centers of industrialization and the railroads—financed by both the government and by private businesses—that supported Japan's economic growth.

was the constant traveling back and forth between them. Being separated from their families was also an unwelcome hardship.

From Rice to Coins

The Tokugawa shogunate tried to preserve a rigid hierarchical order in society. The forces of change worked against them, however, as shown most strongly in the rise of the merchant class and the simultaneous decline of the samurai. In Japanese society, merchants had long been regarded with disdain, especially by the nobility. They were allocated the lowest position among the five traditional social classes, which consisted of the daimyo, samurai, peasants, artisans, and, at the bottom, merchants. Yet when Edo became the Tokugawa capital, the city was already a bustling commercial center with many wealthy merchants.

At this stage, in the early 1600s, rice was still the country's main measure of wealth. The status of a daimyo was determined by the size of his rice crop, and taxes were paid in rice. By the end of the eighteenth

century, gold and silver coins were replacing rice as the means of financial exchange. There were two hundred or more great commercial houses, most based in Edo, whose vast wealth made the samurai's claims of social superiority look ridiculous.

The samurai, who proudly boasted that they had no interest in the sordid world of trade and money, experienced a twofold decline. In the first place, as the power of the shogun increased, so the wars between the great daimyo princes faded away, depriving the samurai of the main reason for their existence. Masterless samurai became a common sight. Secondly, as the money economy developed, so the samurai fell ever deeper into debt to the nonwarrior merchants, whom they despised.

The Suffering of the Peasants

The grievances felt by the great daimyo clans, families of ancient lineage who saw their power and status steadily drain away, became a cause of instability that threatened the dominance of the shogun. So, too, the extreme misery of Japan's rice-growing peasantry threatened shogun authority.

Japan was a mountainous land, in which rice was cultivated in mud-filled paddies, half underwater. The work was backbreaking, requiring the rice to be planted, transplanted, weeded, threshed, winnowed, and polished by hand. This last process required the rice to be hit up to a thousand times with a mallet. The success and stability of the agricultural system depended on containing the peasants in a strictly controlled, feudal framework, where they had no real ownership of their crops.

Any surpluses that the peasants grew were taken from them, and they were subjected to punitive taxation. In addition, they suffered from spectacular crop failures and major famines. In one famine alone, in the middle of the eighteenth century, a million people died.

One consequence of peasant poverty was the custom of *mabiki*, meaning "thinning out." The term derives from the need to thin out rice plants, but it came to refer to the practice of abandoning children outdoors when their families were too poor to raise them. Another consequence was that young girls were commonly sold into prostitution by their parents.

Outbreaks of peasant violence against great landowners became more and more frequent in the last decades of the Tokugawa era, adding to the country's general instability. Even so, the Tokugawa shogunate might have continued for many more years were it not for the arrival of Western merchants. They produced a crisis that the samurai exploited in the hope of reasserting their position. Instead, it led to the downfall of the Tokugawa regime.

Dealing with the West

Like China, Japan had for a long time turned its back on the outside world (*see 4:539*). Most Westerners were banned from setting foot on Japanese soil, let alone trading in the country. Yet, like China, Japan could not avoid the issue of how to deal with an industrialized West that was eager to break down the barriers to trade in Asia.

After the Opium Wars of the early 1840s forced China to open trading relations with the West, European manufacturers looked eagerly at the potential markets offered by Japan. At this time, only the Dutch had a permanent trading colony in Japan, located at Nagasaki. Great Britain had an Asian foothold in Hong Kong, and in 1846 it had been allowed to establish a Christian mission in Okinawa. Russia, which had colonized Siberia and was looking to Japan as a

This hand-colored photograph shows a Japanese child carrying a baby watching women harvest grain in the late nineteenth century.

source of supplies, saw Britain as its main rival in the region.

In July 1853, the residents of Edo were astonished by the arrival in their harbor of four American warships, two of them powered by steam. Under Commodore Matthew Perry, they had come to demand that Japan open its ports to foreign trade. They were soon followed by the arrival of a Russian flotilla at Nagasaki. Within four

Actors portray a daimyo and his servant in this photograph from the 1890s. The daimyo dominated Japanese society until the late nineteenth century.

This suit of armor was made for a samurai knight in the nineteenth century. The samurai attempted to march on the capital to claim power. Instead, they saw their power weakened after the Meiji restoration.

years, Japan's isolation had crumbled. Japan reluctantly signed a series of "unequal treaties" that opened its ports to outside nations, set low import taxes, and exempted foreign citizens in the treaty ports from Japanese law.

The Meiji Restoration

The arrival of foreigners, largely on their own terms, delivered a fatal blow to the tottering Tokugawa shogunate. It was impossible to resist the West, but this fact did not stop the shogun's critics and opponents from rallying behind the cry "Expel the barbarians! Restore the emperor."

The shogun attempted to save himself by making concessions. In 1863, he abolished the hostage system along with the requirement that the daimyo spend half their time in Edo. Soon after, the emperor Komei issued an edict instructing the shogun to expel the foreigners. When the deadline came and nothing had been done, artillery of the Chosu clan opened fire on American, French, and Dutch vessels.

In 1866, the four most powerful daimyo clans of western Japan—the Satsuma and the Chosu above all—buried their ancient rivalries and formed a league to topple the shogun. As their armies advanced on the Edo palace in November 1867, the shogun slipped away to Osaka. By January 1868, the reins of power lay fully in the hands of the fifteen-year-old emperor Meiji. This aristocratic revolution has since become known as the Meiji Restoration.

The emperor's authority was further acknowledged in 1871, when the heads of the four great clans surrendered their vast estates to him, thereby ending the ancient system of feudalism. In return, the emperor established a council of state and appointed several of the old princes to it.

The task ahead of the new government, nominally presided over by the emperor, was daunting. Japan was still a backward country on the fringes of the advanced world, internationally weak and financially nearly bankrupt. The productive energies of its agricultural labor force were being sapped by the heavy demands of a rich merchant class and a parasitic bureaucracy. Above all, there loomed the question of what to do with the samurai.

Disarming the Samurai

The samurai had been the backbone of the movement that overthrew the shogun, but they were also the chief obstacle to modernization. Supporting them drained national finances while contributing nothing to the economy, and they represented an ever-present potential threat to the new order. As a result, they were swiftly brought to heel.

The samurai's hereditary income was cut off, their right to kill commoners at will abolished, and the wearing of swords and topknots was outlawed. Most important of all, military conscription was introduced, replacing the privileged caste of swordsmen with a national army, which came to be called the "nation of samurai." These changes provoked a backlash in the form of a samurai rising in 1877. After heavy fighting, the new order emerged triumphant.

This Japanese print from around 1850 shows an American warship and lists its armaments and technical details. The print also lists distances to foreign countries.

Learning from the West

In the 1870s and 1880s, Japan's new rulers set about reforming the entire state. Despite coming to power under the slogan "Expel the barbarians," they saw that continued isolation stood in the way of progress.

In 1871, a mission headed by the emperor's chief minister, Tomomi Iwakura, went abroad to study Western methods of government and industry. The knowledge he brought back was put to good effect. By the end of the nineteenth century, Japan had created a centralized administration, a modern tax system based on British and French models, a national army, a unified education system, and the foundations of an industrial economy. Between 1868 and 1900, imports of raw materials for Japanese manufactures rose fivefold and the export of manufactured products increased twentyfold. These were the years in which the great financial empires, or zaibatsu, of modern Japan were founded, such as Mitsubishi, which began as a shipbuilding and mining conglomerate.

Democracy, however, was not embraced quite so readily. Although a parliamentary constitution was granted in 1889, Japan continued to be governed in the emperor's name by a small, elite group. The emperor himself was made the object of cult adoration: he was seen as a divine figure who embodied in himself the nation's destiny.

Forging a National Outlook

Worship of the emperor was sustained by Japan's education system and in the way that the state took over the country's religion. In order to ensure acceptance of the new state authority and its sacred emperor, Japan developed a regimented education system. In primary and secondary schools throughout the country, children learned the importance of giving absolute loyalty to the emperor and to Japan's "world mission." Independent thought was all but eliminated in the effort to produce citizens who would place devotion to the state and the throne above everything else. At what were called normal schools—elite schools for future business leaders, managers, and government officials—military discipline was strictly enforced. Pupils were required to do cadet training one day a week.

Equally effective and dramatic was the remarkable state takeover of the Shinto religion. In 1868, most educated Japanese

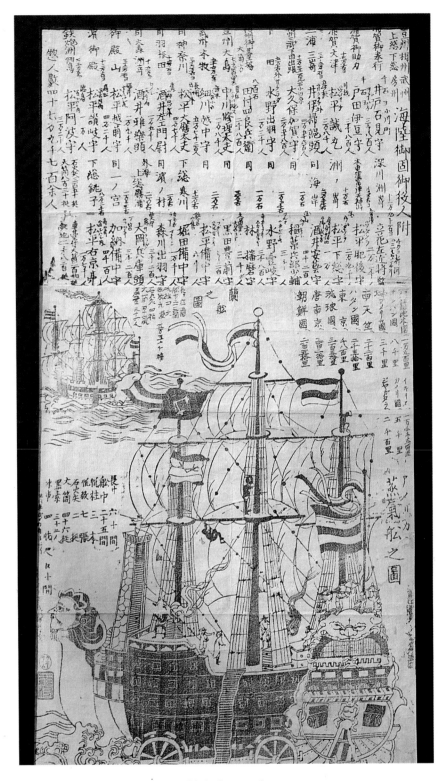

were Buddhists, a few were Christian, and all were influenced to some degree by the ancient Chinese system of Confucianism. Compared with these three great traditions, Shinto was little more than a collection of local superstitions celebrated by Shinto priests at local shrines. Yet the Meiji government set out to impose Shinto on the people as the national creed.

Buddhist temples were pillaged and destroyed, the priests stripped of their authority and robbed of their lands. Every Japanese citizen was required to register at

781

This street scene was photographed in Osaka in the 1890s. The Japanese flag flies above a busy scene of pedestrians and rickshaws.

a Shinto shrine, and an official Department of Divinity was established at the highest level of government. In a statement from 1874, the government went so far as to claim that there was no need for any religious duties beyond worship of the emperor. In short, religion and the state were one and the same.

Japan's Imperial Ambitions

By the 1890s, Japanese potential had never been higher. Japan was determined to become equal to other world powers, and the easiest way to do so was to embark on an aggressive foreign policy. For over a generation, Japanese leaders had looked covetously at Korea, then a virtual colony of China. In 1894, Japan took advantage of an uprising in Korea to send troops into the country. It then refused to withdraw them, and instead declared war on China.

Japan's more modern army won an easy victory that astonished the world. So too did the Treaty of Shimonoseki (1895), by which China agreed to relinquish Taiwan, Port Arthur, and the Liaotung Peninsula to Japan. In the terms of the treaty, China also recognized Korea's independence.

Japanese celebrations were short lived, however. Within a week, a triple intervention by Russia, France, and Germany had compelled Japan to return the Liaotung Peninsula and Port Arthur to China. This humiliation was made worse by the inroads of European powers over the next five years, with Russia seizing Port Arthur. Japan's leaders had learned that military strength, more than anything else, was what counted in international diplomacy.

War with Russia

From 1895, the army and navy came to dominate the Japanese government, which became increasingly eager for foreign conquests. Meanwhile, Japanese achievements continued to gain respect abroad. In 1902, Japan achieved a major triumph by signing an alliance with Britain. Britain recognized that Japan had a special interest in Korea and guaranteed to remain neutral if Japan went to war against Russia. For Japan, this removed the potential threat of the British navy, which was the chief obstacle to its ambitions in the area.

Tension had been simmering between Japan and Russia for some time over their rival claims to Korea and Manchuria. Then, in 1904, Japan launched a surprise attack on the Russian fleet in Port Arthur harbor. The resulting war lasted for eighteen months, and was decided by two great Japanese victories, by the army at Mukden, and by the navy at the Battle of Tsushima. Admiral Togo's surprise destruction of the Russian Baltic fleet at Tsushima made him a national hero and forced the Russians to sue for peace.

Growing Confidence

The terms of the peace settlement gave Japan everything that the triple intervention had taken away in 1895. Even more important, this was the first major victory of an Asian nation over a European enemy in modern times. It announced Japan's arrival on the world stage as the dominant force in Asia.

The first country to feel the effects of Japan's new confidence was its far larger neighbor, China. With the backing of Britain and the United States, Japan set out to replace Russia as the overlord of southern Manchuria. Large numbers of troops were sent to the region and in 1906 a Japanese railway company was established there. The Korean peninsula was next. Japanese troops had never been withdrawn after the 1894 invasion, and in 1910 Japan annexed the country.

Further Military Ambitions

With the European powers distracted by the outbreak of World War I in 1914, Japan flexed its muscles even more. During the early months of the conflict, the Japanese navy took the opportunity to' capture almost all the Pacific islands of the German empire. Japan then went on to present China with an ultimatum, known as the Twenty-One Demands. These included demands that German commercial leases in Shantung province should be transferred to Japan, that China should buy half of its war materials from Japan, that Japanese police should have equal authority with Chinese police in China's major cities, and that China should appoint Japanese economic, political, and military advisers.

The European powers and the United States were taken aback by Japan's audacity. For those who could read the signs, the ultimatum warned that Japan intended to

This *torii* gate stands at the entrance to a Japanese town. A traditional symbol of the Shinto religion, the gate symbolizes the purification of the hearts and minds of those who pass through it.

East and West

The contact between East and West during the nineteenth century sparked a two-way exchange. For the most part, that exchange was one-sided and economic as China and Japan rushed to adopt Western technological advances. It was not entirely one-sided, however, nor was it entirely an economic phenomenon. Cultural, religious, and artistic ideas also passed between the two regions, sometimes with a profound and lasting effect.

Both Japan and China adopted, albeit reluctantly in China's case, Western industrial technology. Arms factories, shipyards, and coal and iron production became primary industries. They were followed by railroads, gunboats, the telegraph, electrification: the fruits of a process of modernization parts of Europe had already been undergoing for a century. Often, Asian businesses began by using imported European machines or European factory managers.

Other changes were less straightforward. In China, determined missionary work gained Christianity a large following alongside the traditional beliefs of Confucianism. An adapted Chinese form of Christianity inspired the Taiping Rebellion of 1850 to 1864. In Europe, meanwhile, religious thinkers were intrigued by the religions of Asia, particularly the Hinduism of India and the Buddhist faith popular in Indochina, in parts of southern China, and in Japan before it was suppressed in favor of Shinto. In Japan, other introductions from European examples ranged from a daily newspaper to military conscription, from a ministry of education to the Western Gregorian calendar, which is still used today.

Perhaps the most extensive exchange of ideas, however, came in the visual arts. Contact with Europe led to the introduction of oil painting in Japan, though it was usually applied to traditional landscapes. Factories mass-produced porcelain for export to Europe. Often, such objects were decorated in an overstated, garish way that had more to do with Western taste than with traditional Japanese values of restraint. Beyond the economic centers, meanwhile, craftsmen continued to produce more refined works.

Europeans and Americans, for their part, grew fascinated with Japanese and, to a lesser extent, Chinese art. The woodcuts of artists such as Hiroshige and Hokusai inspired Western painters such as Paul Gauguin, Henri Toulouse-Lautrec, and Amedeo Modigliani. The famous American architect Frank Lloyd Wright wrote in the early twentieth century of the upheaval this made in the West: "In order to comprehend it at all, we must take a viewpoint unfamiliar to us as a people, and in particular to our artists—the purely aesthetic viewpoint."

Japanese goods also contributed to a wider European vogue for exoticism during the 1880s that also took in African artifacts. Japanese prints and masks decorated living rooms furnished with lac-

Created in 1875 by Utagawa Hiroshige, this print uses the traditional Japanese artform of the woodblock to celebrate the opening of a railroad station in Tokyo. The line between the capital and Yokohama was completed in 1875 with the help of foreign engineers.

quered cabinets, samurai swords, and bamboo parasols. Drug taking became a popular pastime, in an echo of opium addiction in China. Chinese workers from the goldfields and railroads introduced Asian cuisine to the United States, including chop suey, a dish invented in America.

In Japan, meanwhile, the decades after the introduction of Western trade saw a fashion for Western culture. Western furniture, hairstyles, and dress became status symbols that proclaimed a Japanese as modern and forward looking. European musical instruments and music became popular. Collections of songs were published with Japanese lyrics accompanied by traditional Western tunes. The vogue was as short as it was intense. It disappeared within twenty years or so under the weight of increasing Japanese nationalism.

In the late twentieth century, the direction of cultural exchange has been largely from East to West. During the 1960s, for example, radical Western movements were heavily influenced by China's Mao Tse-tung in their experiments in communal living. In the 1980s, Western corporations turned to Japanese examples to learn new management techniques for industry.

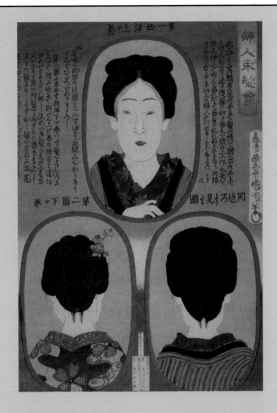

Less than a decade after the Meiji Restoration opened Japan to foreign ideas, this 1877 print showed Japanese women the most up-to-date Western hairstyles.

In this engraving from 1866, a Japanese army officer in traditional clothing looks in amazement at a group of fellow officers who have adopted European trousers and jackets.

785

This photograph shows ships of Russia's Baltic fleet sunk during the Battle of Tsushima in 1905. The fleet sailed halfway around the world to try to join the war against the Japanese but was itself defeated.

make itself overlord, not just of Manchuria, but of the entire East.

The Western allies continued to need Japan's manufactured goods, as well as its shipyards, throughout the war, because their domestic industries were already at full stretch to meet the demands of the conflict. By the time World War I ended in 1919, Japan had not only cleared all its foreign debt but was instead actually owed money by the rest of the world.

By 1919, the prospects for stability and peace in Asia looked positive. Japan, in particular, was set to use the springboard of the war years to enter a phase of strong economic growth. At the same time, however, the militarist and nationalist groups that controlled the government were setting their sights on new objectives that would bring more conflict to the region. When another world war broke out, Japan would not be able to remain aloof again (*see 8:1015*).

Japanese soldiers maneuver a field gun during the war against the Russians in 1904.

THE CONVERTERS

WATCHING THE CONVERTERS

The Second Wave of Industrialization

The Industrial Revolution Reaches Maturity

The effects of the Industrial Revolution were well established by the mid–nineteenth century (*see 5:622*). Industrialization and urbanization had spread from Britain to Western Europe and the United States, carrying all the advantages and disadvantages of modern society (*see 5:625*). Industrial development had become self-perpetuating as companies sought innovations to win a commercial advantage over competitors.

The second wave of industrialization took this process of change further. First, the nature of industry changed as products such as chemicals became important. Second, industry became closely linked with national power. Industry gave a nation economic or strategic strength; in the case of arms or railroads, the effects on the balance of power could be far more practical.

Britain Changes

Britain's prosperity since the early nineteenth century had rested on what historians describe as primary industries: iron, coal,

This colored engraving from 1876 shows various stages of the Bessemer process for converting iron into steel. Lighter and more flexible than iron, steel enabled the building of new structures such as skyscrapers.

and textiles. Coal qualifies as a primary industry because, without it, other industries could not exist. As well as providing fuel for domestic use, coal fueled Britain's transport and metal manufacturing industries. Later, the gas and chemical industries also relied upon coal, the production of which quadrupled between 1830 and 1865. The increased demand led to engineering innovations necessary to exploit more inaccessible coal seams, while those innovations themselves had corollary effects in other industries.

Textiles were a primary industry because cotton spearheaded the dramatic increase in the export trade that confirmed Britain's global economic dominance. Raw cotton imports continued to rise, increasing tenfold throughout the century.

Iron and Steel

As plastic is to the late twentieth century, so iron was to the nineteenth. Adaptable, cheap, and easy to use, iron was the material of choice for a range of industrial and household products, from cast-iron fireplaces to railroad track. Iron was too brittle for some uses, however, though it could be made more flexible by being converted to steel with the introduction of a small amount of carbon.

Steel manufacture remained expensive, however. Although work by Henry Bessemer reduced the price of finished steel, significant advances only came in the early 1870s. The research of William Siemens and the adoption of a new type of open-hearth furnace improved the quality of steel and reduced its cost dramatically. Steel came into wide use for rails, bridges, and shipbuilding. In the United States, the

In this contemporary engraving, Londoners admire the new electric lights built on the Thames Embankment in 1879, the first electric streetlamps in Britain.

This box camera was the first made by the American Kodak company, in 1888. It was supplied with a roll of photographic paper that took 100 shots. The customer then returned the whole camera to Rochester, New York, to develop the photographs

use of relatively light steel girders, along with innovations such as the safety elevator in 1857, allowed for the construction of America's characteristic urban structure, the skyscraper.

Britain Falls Behind

As the nineteenth century went on, Britain failed to capitalize on its early economic dominance. Historians still debate the reason for this failure. Some say that, because Britain was the first country to industrialize, it was later left with older, less efficient machinery and forms of industrial organization while other nations overtook it. In contrast, France, Germany, and the United States could both purchase the latest equipment and learn from earlier mistakes made by British industry. Other historians suggest that British entrepreneurs were ill suited to conducting business in the modern world because British society undervalued commercial and technical skill. Another school of thought holds that Britain's economic performance did not decline at all but simply changed. Its industrial and manufacturing production were overtaken by other countries, but Britain remained dominant in areas such as banking, insurance, and other service industries.

Adapting Industries

As industrialization spread, growing numbers of wage earners demanded products on which to spend their income. The consumer society emerged on an unprecedented scale. Developments in electric lighting, transport, construction, postage, and printing, all contributed to the development of new ways of shopping. The first department store opened in Paris by 1865, while illustrated shopping catalogs offered a huge range of products to consumers who lived far from population centers.

Consumer demand became a major stimulus to the development of secondary industries. A clear example of how quickly a technical innovation became an indispensable part of middle-class life is the spread of photography. A scientific process in the 1850s, photography developed so quickly that by the end of the century Kodak had brought cameras and film developing within the price range of virtually everyone. Kodak's advertising slogan stressed the simplicity of the process: "You push the button, we will do the rest."

Improving Urban Life

In general, urban lives became more comfortable and hospitable in the second half of the century. Reforms created stronger local government for metropolitan areas, while many national governments realized that their earlier policy of laissez-faire, or nonintervention, had created problems of overcrowding and ill health. By the 1850s, many towns and cities were gaining from government-sponsored slum clearance programs that attacked such problems.

One of the most famous examples of urban replanning came in the French capital, Paris. In the 1850s and 1860s, Georges-Eugène Haussmann (1809–1891) remodeled the city under the emperor Napoleon III (*see 5:657*). He drove broad, straight boulevards through the mass of small, twisting streets, connecting the city's railroad stations and for the first time made it easy and quick to cross the city. Haussmann built new parks, improved street lighting, and built sidewalks that encouraged the opening of cafes and stores and the rejuvenation of urban life. While improved communications stimulated the Paris economy, the new roads had another purpose: they

This detail from an 1890 photograph shows a woman demonstrating the use of a Kodak box camera. 789

The Gare St-Lazare, painted by the famous Impressionist painter Claude Monet during the 1870s, shows one of the stations in Paris that served the French provinces. Many European stations employed modern building techniques to create vast steel-and-glass roofs.

were more difficult for rebels to barricade than smaller streets.

Haussmann's improvements to the Paris water supply were echoed in many municipalities, as celebrated in many European cities by fountains dating from this period. Where city authorities were reluctant to enact basic public health measures, catastrophe still occurred. As late as 1892, a cholera epidemic in the German city of Hamburg killed ten thousand people.

The arrival of cheap and reliable forms of street lighting gradually made urban living safer and more pleasant. Many early systems were fueled by coal gas, supplies of which were so cheap and plentiful that there was little stimulus to develop other means of lighting, thus indirectly inhibiting the growth of the electricity industry.

Domestic life also eventually profited from improvements in lighting and heating, though gaslighting only appeared in London homes around the 1890s. The American author Edgar Allan Poe had condemned the new form of lighting decades earlier: "Its harsh and unsteady light offends. No one having both brains and eyes will use it."

Electric lighting, demonstrated by the American inventor Thomas Edison in 1878 only really became popular after the end of World War I forty years later. Although manufacturers such as the American Westinghouse and the German Siemens pioneered electrical appliances for cooking, heating, and cleaning in the 1890s, they were slow to become popular. Many people were afraid of this mysterious, invisible form of energy and, in any case, most of those who could afford the new inventions could also afford servants to perform the tasks, so had little reason to buy.

The Spread of the Railroads

The second wave of industrialization stimulated railroad building, which became a significant indicator of economic health. Between 1850 and 1870, Europe's railroads expanded from roughly 15,000 miles of track to nearly 66,000 miles. Even in the less industrialized countries of southern Europe, railroads grew rapidly. American expansion was even more impressive, from 10,000 miles to approximately 56,000 miles. Services became regularized and quicker. Goods and passengers traveled at

speeds that would not be improved upon for nearly a century to come.

Like coal and iron, railroads had an important influence on further industrialization. In France, for example, the government intervened to raise investment for railroads when they began to lag behind those of Great Britain and Prussia. By the 1848 revolution, only 2,000 miles of track were open, and a significant share of track under construction was financed solely by the government. By 1870, however, France possessed an impressive system of trunk, or main, lines that had been taken into private control. By the outbreak of World War I in 1914, France still had 7,000 miles of track less than Germany.

Industrialization and the State
The French anxiety to develop their infrastructure illustrated an important aspect of later industrialization. Technological advance was intimately connected with national strength. France's anxiety was fueled by fear of Germany, where Prussia led a rapid expansion of railroads from 500 miles of track in 1844 to 1,500 miles four years later and 3,500 miles by 1860.

In Germany, unlike France, the railroad had enthusiastic support from all parts of society. Landowners saw that it could transport agricultural products to markets quickly. Industrialists saw railroads as essential to the economies of scale and access to markets required by a modern economy. Above all, the Prussian military realized the strategic potential of the railroad long before other nations'. Under the influence of the chief of staff, Helmuth von Moltke, the Prussians built lines to serve military needs, linking urban centers to potential flashpoints on Germany's western and eastern borders (*see 5:662*).

Transport Improvements
Railroads were not the only area of transport that improved significantly. European and American cities were transformed by mass transit systems, which were prompted by and also helped to encourage the emergence of a new type of worker, the commuter. Tramways offered a cheap and relatively quick form of urban transport. Originally pulled by horses, by the end of the century trams were usually electrically powered by overhead lines.

A boy with a goat-drawn cart is dwarfed by Angel's Curve, a section of elevated railroad tracks in New York City, in this photograph from around 1883. Much of the New York El was later dismantled in favor of the subway, which occupied less space and was not so unsightly.

Steamships line the dockside in the port of Calcutta, India. Among other benefits, the development of improved shipping made it easier for imperial nations, such as Britain, to maintain contact with their overseas colonies.

As congestion grew in city streets, London invested in an underground railroad, or subway. The initiative was soon followed in other European cities and eventually in America, Asia, and Australia. Some cities solved the same problem by building elevated tracks over rather than under the street. New York had the first steam-powered line in 1871, while Chicago had the first electric line in 1895.

Steamships became faster and more economical after the middle of the century, and the number in service grew tenfold between 1850 and 1870. Journey times halved and were no longer dependent upon the weather. Such developments enabled

Looking nervous, a Frenchwoman tries out an early version of a tricycle in a Paris park in the 1890s.

the growth of an international communications network by creating reliable postal services. With other innovations, such as refrigeration, they also allowed Western nations access to new sources of food: cocoa from Africa, bananas and beef from Latin America, lamb and dairy products from Australasia.

Transport and Freedom

Toward the end of the nineteenth century, the automobile industry became significant, thanks to the lead of the German firms Daimler and Benz. The development of a British motor industry, meanwhile, was retarded by a law that kept automobile speeds low and required that someone walk in front of a vehicle carrying a red flag to warn pedestrians. The British motor vehicle industry remained smaller than those in France, Germany, and the United States for some time to come.

Although the automobile would become the world's dominant form of transport, it had less immediate effect near the end of

the nineteenth century than another new form of transport, the bicycle. The first modern bicycles began to appear in Paris in the 1860s. Technical advances and increased demand saw a bicycling craze on both sides of the Atlantic in the 1890s.

The bicycle had significant social effects. The availability of cheap models allowed people to travel further to work, even when public transport was unavailable. Above all, having an independent means of travel allowed middle-class women new forms of freedom and escape from the confines of the home.

Cycling even affected the way people dressed. Reformers such as the American Amelia Bloomer (1818–1894) had argued since the midcentury that women should adopt garments with legs as a more practical way to dress than skirts and dresses. Such clothes—known as Bloomers—had been dismissed as scandalous, as they showed the shape of women's legs. Now, increasing numbers of women began to wear knickerbockers as they cycled.

This early Daimler automobile from Germany, photographed in 1906, belonged to the British king Edward VII. The British motor industry lagged behind those of Germany, France, and the United States.

793

This contemporary engraving shows the Krupp 14-inch (355 mm) gun on display at the Paris Exhibition of 1867. Only a few years later, in the Franco-Prussian War, similar guns bombarded French cities, including Paris, into surrender.

National Specialization

The chemical industry that developed in the second half of the nineteenth century promised a means of maintaining dynamic industrial expansion. Chemical fertilizers increased agricultural production to feed the new urban populations. Chemical dyes enabled the textile industry to offer a wider range of higher-value goods to a larger market. Because the chemical industry did not develop until numerous countries were already industrialized, there was little of the common development seen in earlier industries such as coal.

Britain, for example, concentrated on the production of soda ash, which was used in the glassmaking, soap, and bleaching industries. Britain also had a significant lead in various areas of the food processing and brewing industries. The United States, meanwhile, led the world in the production of sulphuric acid and phosphates. Germany became dominant in the pharmaceutical and, above all, dyeing industries. By 1890, nine-tenths of the world's artificial dyes were German.

The chemical industry also spearheaded the development of research and development as a way to increase production, markets, and profits. Laboratory work led to the adaptation of established raw materials to new uses, such as the use of rubber in car and bicycle tires.

The Arms Industry

Industrial development revolutionized the face of warfare. The Napoleonic Wars of the opening decade of the century involved relatively small armies and had comparatively little effect upon the general population (*see 5:598*). The American Civil War (1861–1865) was partly decided by the Union's industrial superiority, particularly in its railroads (see *5:679*). By the Franco-Prussian War (1870–1871), industrial production and superior weapons had become as important as military prowess. The French developed the chassepot rifle and the mitrailleuse, an early machine gun; the Prussians possessed the needle gun and outstanding artillery. In 1867, the arms company Krupp displayed a 14-inch (355 mm) siege gun at the Paris Exhibition. Nearly five years later, the Prussians used the same weapon to bombard Paris into surrender.

The Prussians also had a decisive advantage when it came to moving their armies. Six railroad lines led to the frontier with France, while the French only had two in the other direction. While the Prussians mobilized nearly 500,000 men in just over a fortnight, France managed only 200,000.

A Model of Industrialization

The unified Germany whose creation Prussia engineered in 1871 rapidly developed a modern industrial infrastructure to

This painting from the 1870s shows the Excelsior Iron Works in New York. The United States had vast supplies of iron ore in the Appalachians, Colorado, and Michigan's upper peninsula.

rival the other European powers. There were several reasons for this success. State intervention and a strong banking sector encouraged the development of major industries by making easier the significant capital investment needed to buy increasingly expensive industrial plant. Germany also benefited from industrializing comparatively late, capitalizing on established rather than experimental technologies.

German industrial development was supported by a sophisticated system of scientific and technical education that produced engineers and workers. Aggressive German munitions interests channeled industrial might to military and naval improvements, which in turn supported a growing commit-

This photograph from the early 1900s shows young children on their way to school in Homestead, Pennsylvania, one of the many steel towns that grew up around the conversion of iron to steel.

795

The Brooklyn Bridge, photographed around 1900, was built over the East River between Brooklyn and Manhattan between 1869 and 1883. Then the world's largest suspension bridge, it was the first structure built using cables made from steel.

ment to acquiring an empire that would provide raw materials and marketplaces for German industry. Such considerations partly prompted German involvement in the scramble for Africa in the last decades of the century, when European powers established colonies on the continent (*see 6:822*). Meanwhile, rapid development brought some of the ills of industrialization: vast slums developed in the German capital, Berlin.

A Separate Case: Russia

Industrial developments remained at the mercy of a nation's social system. Russia remained a largely feudal country with little means of raising finance capital (*see 5:694*). Many of the factories and businesses that grew up at the end of the nineteenth century were owned by Europeans seeking new regions for investment.

Resentment of this foreign dominance also retarded economic progress. Russia had nevertheless taken the first steps toward industrialization with the introduction of railroads and heavy industry. Just as in the West earlier in the century, Russia possessed cruder forms of manufacturing but still lacked the more sophisticated precision industries that now characterized the rest of the continent.

Europe's Industry Falters

By 1900, European industry was already being overtaken by the United States, buoyed by rich supplies of raw materials and ingenious, inventive citizens. Within two decades, the development of ever-more efficient means of waging war would leave Europe's economies devastated by World War I (*see 7:897*).

Late-Nineteenth-Century Society in the West

The Dominance of the Middle Classes

The late nineteenth century in Western Europe and the United States saw the continuation of social developments sparked by the Industrial Revolution (*see 5:625*). Among the significant changes was the emergence of subtle distinctions of class as important factors in social life. People saw themselves as having distinct class identities, whose priorities conflicted with other classes'. This perspective was particularly true of the middle class, which was anxious to distinguish itself from the working class. Equally important was the idea that people could move between classes by "improving" themselves or falling from grace.

Earlier ways of dividing society, such as the estates of the early modern world, assumed that people would remain in the estate in which they were born.

Neither the middle class nor the working class were uniform. The middle class included wealthy urban business leaders, country schoolteachers, and parsons. It also included a significant new component in white-collar workers, who were often working class in origin. This group included factory supervisors, secretaries, shop clerks, and minor bureaucrats. Whatever its origins, the white-collar labor force was solidly middle class in its aspirations.

This portrayal of a family Christmas, produced in England around 1900, depicts the ideal of family life and domestic harmony that shaped the ambitions of Europe's middle classes.

Queen Victoria cradles one of her great grandchildren in an 1895 photograph intended to portray the royal family as embodying the attitudes of their middle-class subjects. The portrait includes three future English kings: Victoria's son, on the left, became Edward VII; her grandson, on the right, became George V; the baby grew up to become Edward VIII.

Middle-Class Family Life

During the late nineteenth century, the lifestyle of the middle classes set the tone for society. At the center of their lives was the family, with marriage as a crucial social and economic building block. Achieving an advantageous and respectable marriage was a major goal for both men and women. Within the family, the two sexes had different but complementary roles. The man was expected to achieve respectability and social prominence through participation in business and government. The woman was perceived as the "angel in the house," who provided comfort and moral guidance and maintained a private retreat away from the toils of the unstable business world.

The middle-class father presided over his family like the head of a firm. He controlled most of his wife's property, and he exercised considerable influence over his unmarried daughters. His sons depended upon him for an allowance and for the private schooling that would enable them to advance socially and economically.

A wife's task was to keep the household running smoothly. She was also the person primarily responsible for the moral guidance of her children. Supposedly free from the passions that swayed the male sex, women possessed a natural moral authority. As part of the effort to distinguish themselves from their social inferiors, middle-class women did not go out to work. Women had to find their lives' purpose in being wives and mothers. Even Britain's Queen Victoria, the most famous woman of the time, projected an image that reflected the middle-class virtues of domesticity and motherhood. In reality, many middle-class mothers spent little time with their children, who were raised mainly by nursemaids and governesses. Boys were commonly sent to boarding schools.

The Social Duties of Women

Much of a middle-class woman's day was spent in the company of women of the same social rank. Economically secure women participated in a round of social engagements, in which they either called on acquaintances or notified them as to when they would be "at home" and available for visiting. Strict etiquette dictated who could call on whom and when. The round of visiting was part of an elaborate ritual for maintaining the appearance of respectability, a burden which fell largely on the shoulders of women.

Women were praised for their abilities as graceful hostesses. They were taught social graces, such as drawing, painting, singing, or playing the piano. A middle-class woman would often know little more than a smattering of math, geography, history, and a foreign language. In contrast, her brothers or sons would usually receive an expensive private education to prepare them for business or a position in government.

Respectable women were bound by other constraints. They did not, for example, go out without a chaperone, who might be a male family member, a female friend, or a maid. One European dance manual of 1880 declared: "A lady should not attend a public ball without an escort, nor should she promenade the ball room alone; in fact, no lady should be left unattended."

The Middle-Class Home

Middle-class houses and furnishings strove to express the values of their owners. Furniture was solidly built and often heavily decorated with gilt, fringes, and other ornamentation. Rooms were crowded with furniture, art objects, wall hangings, and other possessions that expressed ideals of comfort and luxury. Exotic imports such as oriental rugs and china were highly valued as home decorations.

The household itself was rigidly structured. At its head stood the husband, followed by the wife as a kind of glorified housekeeper and the servants in positions of descending rank below her. Even poor middle-class families tried to keep at least one servant to confirm their social status.

The Shrinking Family

During the second half of the nineteenth century, families became generally smaller. One of the reasons was that more people learned about contraception as a means of birth control. Another reason lay in the growth of urbanization. While farming families were traditionally large because children were useful as help with agricultural work, town dwellers did not follow this pattern. Even poor families were prevented from sending children to work by strict child labor laws. Children became a drain on the family finances rather than a source of income. In place of the agricultural family with eight or nine children, the middle-class urban family shrank to an average of only two or three offspring.

For middle-class women, fewer children meant even fewer responsibilities in the home. To counter the boredom of empty days and as an expression of genuine sympathy, women became increasingly involved in charity work and causes such as temperance reform, education of the poor, and child welfare.

There were a few career opportunities open to women, particularly as teachers. For most middle-class women, however, paid employment remained socially unacceptable. Volunteer work was more acceptable because it was an extension of the female role of moral guide and nurturer.

The Working-Class Woman

If middle-class women found their lives restricted and boring, women of the working class had many more difficulties. They often bore more children because contraceptive devices remained expensive and contraception itself was widely seen as immoral. Many working-class women were almost constantly pregnant throughout their childbearing years.

Like the middle-class wife, her working-class counterpart was responsible for the general maintenance of the household. She

was usually given a portion of her husband's weekly wages, from which she had to house, feed, and clothe the entire family. Women often deprived themselves to make ends meet for the sake of their children. Their husbands, meanwhile, often did as they liked with the rest of the money.

In addition to these domestic responsibilities, many working-class women had little or no choice but to find employment. Women worked in factories in growing numbers throughout the century. Many also worked for an employer at home, doing what was known as homework or piecework. This work was notoriously badly paid, since the workers were not paid for time worked but instead by, for example, how many matchboxes were glued. Children might often help their mother in these laborious tasks, which would some-

Typical of the detailed, gilded furniture popular in contemporary Europe, this sideboard was created by an Italian designer in 1851.

This table laid for dinner in the mid–nineteenth century illustrated a cookbook published at the end of the century. Europe's middle and upper classes regularly enjoyed large meals of many courses, prepared by their household servants. Cookbooks became more popular as servants became rarer and women learned to cook for themselves.

times require making thousands of articles just to earn a relative pittance.

By far the largest occupation for young working-class women was in domestic service, working as cooks or chambermaids in the houses of others. Many of these young women became the prey of unscrupulous employers who demanded, or tricked them into granting, sexual favors.

Other desperate young women turned to prostitution, which the anonymity of city life encouraged. Prostitutes were in great demand among certain middle-class men, who might have regarded lower-class women as more accessible and sexually provocative than the "ladies" they wished to marry. Informal moral standards differed for men and women. A middle-class husband might demand fidelity from his wife and chastity from his daughters while he secretly visited brothels.

Educational Reform

The nineteenth century was a period of great educational reform in Europe and the United States, which produced the world's first mass reading public. Reformers strove to provide all children with a primary education, which would give them basic skills in reading, writing, and elementary math, whatever their social background. In France, for example, important changes affecting the working class included the introduction of compulsory elementary schooling for boys and girls in the 1880s.

Educational reformers were motivated by the hope that literacy would help the poor help themselves and would also help create a better, more productive workforce. Many new schools were founded, causing a rapid expansion of the teaching profession. The demand for teachers was so great that women soon achieved a prominence in elementary-school education denied to them in other professions. It was only in the early twentieth century that most children went on to high school.

Charity and Religion

Europe's middle classes echoed some of the beliefs once associated with America's early Puritans. They emphasized the values of thrift and hard work and the reform of society. Many middle-class people condemned the terrible conditions that industrialism inflicted on the poor. Social commentators, such as the British reformer Thomas Carlyle, denounced the values of capitalism and the grinding poverty it caused. As their sense of their own respectability and power increased, the middle classes also sought to reform other ranks of society. One of their favorite causes was temperance. Alcohol was a growing problem in society, especially among people weighed down by the poverty of urban life. In 1850, there were 1,200 drinking houses in Manchester alone.

Advances in Medicine

Medical science was another area that made huge strides forward. Among the drugs discovered during the nineteenth century were morphine, quinine, atropine, codeine, and iodine. Several virulent diseases were conquered from the 1870s onward, including scarlet fever, diphtheria, whooping cough, and typhoid. Cholera was eliminated by improvements in public sanitation. The number of hospitals grew steadily, as did the status of physicians as a professional class. Hospitals not only provided care for more patients but also created greater opportunities for training new doctors. Meanwhile, general anesthetics and antiseptics came into wide use, reducing the risk of a patient dying while undergoing surgery.

Despite these advances in medicine, doctors still had a poor understanding of the causes of many diseases and a limited ability to fight them. After 1880, however, the mortality rate began to fall rapidly in advanced countries. One consequence of this development was to reinforce the division in Europe between West and East, where life expectancy remained relatively low.

Sanitation and Hygiene

Among the principal causes of disease were poor levels of sanitation and hygiene, especially in towns and cities. Many people believed that bathing was unhealthy, so taking a bath was a rare event among all classes. When people did bathe, it was an unpleasant, time-consuming process. Water had to be heated on the stove, and thus it was difficult to fill a bath. As a result, most people used a basin or a washstand to keep themselves clean. Among the poorer classes, water had to be carried into the house two or three times a week from a street pump shared by twenty or thirty families on a block. The water supply was irregular at the best of times.

Toilets, or water closets, were still rare, even among the richest families. Most households used buckets, called privy pails, some of which were simply emptied into the streets. Streets were often filthy,

with raw sewage running down open drains. Because drains were made out of stone, they often leaked, especially into the dwellings of the lower classes. The middle classes often chose to build their homes on

This luxurious canopy bed in the neoclassical style was created for the 1876 Philadelphia Centennial Exposition and later mass-produced in the United States.

This 1898 certificate showed that its holder had sworn to give up alcohol. Temperance was a favorite cause of European and American middle-class women.

801

The general office of a steelworks in 1890 is staffed by clerks typical of the new breed of white-collar workers who became increasingly important and numerous in the second half of the century.

elevated sites. Their sewage simply filtered down into the lower-lying areas, where the working classes lived.

Sewage that flowed through the drains eventually reached a nearby river. Raw sewage floated on the surface of many of Europe's rivers. During the Great Stink of 1858, the Thames's unbearable stench forced the British Parliament to abandon its riverside premises. In response, engineers pioneered the building of sewers for the safe disposal of urban waste. It was one of the great accomplishments of nineteenth-century sanitary engineering.

Many people still failed to perceive the connection between polluted drinking water and disease, so there were regular outbreaks of cholera and typhoid across Europe. The last cholera epidemic occurred in 1899. These epidemics usually had high mortality rates. The poor were most at risk from a lack of hygiene. Harsh living conditions and a poor diet undermined their health, so they were especially vulnerable to problems brought on by food prepared or stored in unsanitary conditions. Stomachaches, indigestion, and other symptoms of food poisoning were common afflictions of the period. Toward the end of the century, the bad health of the poor became obvious when European

countries had difficulties in recruiting for their armies new troops who were actually fit for military service.

Life in the City

The Industrial Revolution reshaped both the landscape of Europe and the lifestyles of countless men and women. The introduction of mass production and the factory system compelled millions of people to migrate from the countryside to small towns and cities. By about 1900, about half of Western Europe's population lived in urban areas. In the most heavily industrialized countries, such as Britain and Germany, the proportion of town dwellers was considerably higher.

Europe's rapidly growing cities were characterized by great wealth and splendor as well as miserable squalor. Prosperous Europeans, having no desire to live near inner-city slums, took advantage of improved public transport and commuter railroads to build suburbs where they lived in fine houses. They also commissioned splendid buildings such as city halls, stock exchanges, museums, and opera houses to celebrate their achievements. In contrast, the working classes lived in cramped, often ramshackle dwellings. In France, family homes were divided into apartments that

might provide only one room per family. In the manufacturing cities of Britain, rows of tiny houses were built close to the factories. In New York, three-quarters of the two million inhabitants crammed into only 43,000 tenements. Old houses in other cities were subdivided into cramped apartments for rapidly expanding populations. Families of up to eight people frequently lived in two small rooms or three at most.

Well-to-do Parisians explore the sewers of Paris in a specially constructed vessel. The sewage systems built in the late nineteenth century were hailed as masterpieces of civil engineering and celebrated as monuments to human ingenuity.

This present-day view shows the Vienna State Opera House, built between 1861 and 1869. Opera houses and theaters were built in many cities around the same time to cater to the relatively affluent and leisured urban population.

Sentiment and Sympathy

This embroidered valentine dates from the nineteenth century. Although valentine messages dated from some 300 years earlier, it was only in the 1800s that mass production made them as familiar as they are today.

The late nineteenth century was a time of great contrasts. The middle-class values that dominated life were governed by strict codes of behavior. This was the period when the saying arose that "children should be seen and not heard." Public displays of temper, emotion, or affection were frowned upon as being in bad taste. Restraint and modesty dominated social behavior. It was said that some people were so prudish that they covered up classical statues of naked bodies.

This stereotyped view of the period gives only one side of the story. People's inner lives found means of expression that were far less restrained than might be expected, particularly in an excessive display of self-indulgent sentimentality. One focus for this sentimentality was death, a familiar aspect of the period because mortality rates remained relatively high and untimely deaths were common. After Prince Albert, the German husband of the British queen Victoria, died in 1861, his widow wore heavy black mourning for the remaining forty years of her life.

Children, who were idealized as symbols of innocence in contrast to the evils of industrial society, often died early from diseases, such as consumption. In France, a fashion arose among middle-class families to photograph dead children as souvenirs. Sometimes the bodies were posed in elaborate sets that portrayed the child's welcome into heaven.

Children's deaths became a popular subject for literature, where they provided readers with channels for emotional release often denied them in everyday life. The English author Charles Dickens specialized in tear-jerking deathbed scenes in his novels, which, as was common at the time, were published in serial form. The death of Little Nell, the young heroine of *The Old Curiosity Shop,* caused a huge sensation on both sides of the Atlantic in 1841. Crowds were said to have gathered on New York's quayside to await the liner bringing copies of the latest installment from Britain. As the ship docked, they called up to the passengers, "Is Little Nell dead?"

A similarly sentimental view of children was presented in Charles Kingsley's novel *The Waterbabies,* of 1863. Kingsley's tale portrayed exploited working-class children escaping their miserable lives to join a race of innocent babies who lived free of care in streams and ponds. In the United States, novels such as *Little Women* by Louisa May Alcott and Joel Chandler Harris's *Uncle Remus* portrayed sentimentalized views of American life.

Sentiment did not only extend to children. Attitudes to animals had begun to change in the first half of the century, and the Royal Society for the Prevention of Cruelty to Animals was formed in Britain in 1824. France followed in 1845, and most Western countries soon adopted measures to protect animals. The British artist Edwin Landseer painted popular portrayals of animals suffering human emotions, such as grief. Among the artist's emotive subjects, for example, was a sheepdog sitting sorrowfully beside

an empty chair. Landseer called the painting *The Old Shepherd's Chief Mourner*. In the 1870s, Anna Sewell wrote the classic children's story *Black Beauty*, an autobiography of a horse, which aimed to prevent the mistreatment of animals.

The late nineteenth century also saw the establishment of many sentimental traditions that still shape modern lives. Although Christmas is an ancient religious festival, its familiar shape only dates from the Victorian age. The first Christmas card was printed in Britain in 1843. Soon afterward, the idea was taken up by a store owner in Albany, New York. The Christmas tree, long popular in Germany, spread to other countries partly thanks to the influence of Prince Albert.

In both Europe and America, a parallel to sentimentality came in the emergence of melodrama. This was a type of play or novel that revolved around a highly dramatic conflict between good and evil in which good always triumphed after numerous cliff-hanging scenes. Although the characters were two dimensional and the plots sensational, melodrama was a popular and prolific form. Its exaggerated gestures and conflicts were later adopted by Hollywood for early silent movies.

In novels, melodrama saw the emergence of the thriller as a popular literary form. The English author Wilkie Collins came up with fiction's first detective novel in *The Moonstone*. Later, the Sherlock Holmes stories of Arthur Conan Doyle achieved such worldwide popularity that, when the author killed off his detective in 1893, public pressure had him brought back to life. Doyle spent much of his later life on a project that was typical of the late nineteenth century in its sentimental eccentricity. He tried unsuccessfully to prove the veracity of a photograph that reputedly showed two young girls playing with fairies.

The Flower of the Flock, an engraving based on a painting by a British artist from around 1890, shows a father cuddling his sick daughter, who does not have long to live. The pity of the child's death is emphasized by her parents' helpless concern and by their idealized, clean and modest home, by which the artist illustrates that the girl's illness is no fault of her family.

805

In this photograph from Minnesota around 1900, the women hold tennis rackets while the young boy grasps a baseball bat, a sign of the increasing mass participation in sports.

Leisure and Popular Culture

The self-confident middle classes took a leading role in transforming the concept of leisure in the second half of the century. For them, leisure had to be both respectable and productive. Walking became a popular activity, providing both exercise and contact with nature.

Middle-class business leaders, officials, and local philanthropists established parks in towns to counteract the spread of urbanization. New York's Central Park, in the heart of Manhattan, opened in 1876. Wealthy people also set up clubs where they could indulge new hobbies such as golf, cricket, rugby, and tennis. Music halls and theaters were also popular diversions. Many churches built their own halls for parishioners to conduct amateur dramatics.

For the middle classes, vacations became increasingly common. Thanks to better railroads and roads, vacations to the seaside were affordable for families of even modest means. After 1850, the demand for seaside accommodation rose dramatically. Atlantic City's boardwalk was built in New Jersey in 1870, and many British resorts erected amusement piers jutting out into the ocean.

Not all leisure activities were pursued away from the home. The nineteenth century was the heyday of novelists such as Charles Dickens and Anthony Trollope in England, Tolstoy and Dostoevsky in Russia,

Balzac and Zola in France. Their writings, often serialized in newspapers and magazines, were popular with all levels of society (*see 6:845*). Growing literacy among the working classes brought a significant increase in the consumption of popular fiction. Equally successful were cheap, mass-circulation newspapers such as *Le Petit Journal* of Paris and the *Daily Mail* and *Daily Express* of London. Not everyone approved. Many intellectuals criticized the flood of popular writing. Social and cultural critics lamented the poor taste of the reading public and accused journals and newspapers of contributing to a decline of morals.

The Search for a Better Life

In response to the problems of European society, a huge tide of people emigrated in search of a better life. Between 1846 and 1932, more than fifty million Europeans moved to the United States, Canada, Australia, South Africa, Brazil, and Argentina.

Up to the 1850s, most of the emigrants were from Great Britain—particularly Ireland—Germany, and Scandinavia. After 1865, the majority were from southern and eastern Europe. A tiny fraction of the newcomers were professionals or entrepreneurs. Most were working people, tired of the poverty, squalor, and lack of opportunity in their homelands. For them, the New World's promise of a better life, better wages, and cheap land was irresistible.

This certificate of membership of the Amalgamated Society of Engineers was designed in 1851. On the left, a worker rejects Mars, the Roman god of war; on the right, another worker is honored by the goddess of peace. The portraits show famous British inventors above scenes illustrating the various trades followed by union members.

The Rise of Socialism

Workers' Politics in the Industrialized World

Four years after the final defeat of Napoleon in 1815 brought peace to Europe, a crowd of 7,000 people gathered at St. Peter's Fields, outside Manchester in northern England. They had turned out to hear a famous radical orator, Henry Hunt, speak in favor of parliamentary reforms that would give more political power to ordinary people. The authorities sent in mounted troops to dispel the meeting. Although Hunt asked his listeners to leave peaceably, the soldiers charged into the crowd, lashing out with their swords. They killed eleven people and injured another

This engraving of the Peterloo massacre was published soon after the event, in 1819. The violent suppression of a peaceful meeting demonstrated the fear of radical politics shared by governments throughout Europe after the close of the French Revolution.

400. The event was dubbed the Peterloo massacre, an ironic reference to the army's victory over Napoleon at Waterloo. The incident became a lasting symbol of the lack of political power of ordinary people.

The Spread of Radical Ideas

The French Revolution had preached the gospel of "liberty, equality, and fraternity." In its aftermath, ruling classes everywhere in Europe saw it as their duty to stop the spread of such dangerous ideas (*see 5:606*). As the nineteenth century unfolded, however, it became impossible to resist the tide of reform. Industrialization and urbanization altered how people lived so dramatically that governments had to cope with new social and economic problems (*see 5:625*). New organizations such as pressure groups and labor organizations emerged to influence governments, demanding a better life for the mass of the people.

The reformers faced many barriers. The ruling classes wanted to preserve their own power. Europe's governors believed that relatively few people with high incomes and valuable property should vote in elections and that ordinary people were too ignorant to have any say in government. The latter argument meant that the right to education, too, was on the radical agenda.

A more general philosophical obstacle to reform concerned the nature of government itself. The dominant philosophy of many reforming liberals was laissez-faire, a French phrase meaning "let people be." This view argued that government should not interfere in the economy, which should be shaped only by supply and demand. Liberals did not believe unemployment or the inequality of wealth between rich and poor to be problems that governments could solve, even if they wanted to.

The word *socialism* appeared in France in the 1830s to describe reformers who opposed laissez-faire. They and their successors believed that free trade benefited mainly the rich. Instead, they called for governments to create more equal social structures in which the division of oppressor and oppressed would not exist and in which property would be distributed more fairly or abolished. While liberalism had appealed largely to Europe's middle classes who sought legal and political equality, socialism appealed more to the growing legions of Europe's workers.

The Beginnings of Change

Political exclusion was not simply a matter of wealth. Most European states had an established national religion—the United States, where church and state were separate—was an exception—and people outside that church were often deprived of civic rights. The democratic movement aimed to end such discrimination. Britain's Roman Catholics were allowed to sit in Parliament in 1829 for the first time since the English Civil War (*see 2:243*). In the 1830s, Protestants such as Baptists and Unitarians gained nearly equal political and civic rights with members of the official church. Britain's Jews had to wait another three decades, however. Other advances for liberty came through the abolition of slavery

The daughters of factory workers take a dancing class at New Lanark, an ideal community established by Robert Owen in Scotland in the 1820s. Such experiments prefigured the utopian visions of much socialist and communist thought.

in Europe and, later, in the United States. The serfs of Russia gained their freedom in 1861.

Britain's Primacy

The most significant advances in the first half of the century took place in Great Britain, thanks to its history of parliamentary government and its early industrialization. The ban on trade unions—workers' organizations devoted to improving conditions and pay—was lifted in 1825, and the unions were given the right to go on strike in support of their demands.

In 1832, the British Parliament passed the Great Reform Act, which marked an important extension in parliamentary democracy. Before 1832, parliamentary seats were still distributed on the pattern of a largely vanished rural Britain. Some members of Parliament represented "rotten boroughs" where no one any longer lived. Citizens of the crowded new manufacturing towns, meanwhile, had no representation. The Reform Act partly remedied this injustice and gave the vote to more people, including the middle classes, traders, and factory owners.

Britain did not become a modern democracy overnight. By today's standards, the electorate was still a small elite. Only one man in thirty had the vote and no women. In France, where an extension of the vote also took place in the early 1830s, only one in 200 men was allowed to vote.

In *The Water Babies*, a popular 1863 story in which working children become members of a blessed race of water babies, author Charles Kingsley imagined a miraculous solution for society's ills.

Taken by an anonymous photographer around 1903, this picture of children working at a U.S. coal mine is evidence that conditions for many child laborers had not significantly improved during the nineteenth century.

The Chartists

In Britain, a radical pressure group began organizing protests against the poor laws, which placed the unemployed in workhouses (*see 5:632*), and in favor of a maximum ten-hour day. The group developed into the Chartist movement.

The Chartists took their name from a charter adopted by the London Men's Working Association in 1836. Disappointed by the 1832 Reform Act, the association demanded the vote for all adult males, secret ballots, and the dropping of the requirement that members of Parliament should own property. The early 1840s were years of high unemployment and high food prices. Economic hardship drove people into the ranks of the Chartists. As the economy improved, however, the movement lost impetus and withered. It held its last public meeting in 1848. None of its demands were granted by Parliament.

Inspired by liberalism and nationalism, revolutions swept across Europe in 1848 (*see 5:613*). The old order soon reasserted itself, however. Some permanent gains had been won. Prussia had a partially elected assembly, or diet, for example. The year 1848 also marked the publication by Karl Marx and Friedrich Engels of a profoundly influential tract, *The Communist Manifesto* (*see 6:812*). This work argued that the world's workers would eventually overthrow existing forms of government.

Marx was not alone in preaching socialism or social systems based on collective ownership rather than private property. Thinkers such as the Welshman Robert Owen (1771–1858), who set up model societies at New Lanark in Scotland and New Harmony in the United States, argued for a society in which property should be held in common by the people and society organized around the principle of cooperation rather than competition. "Property is theft" wrote the French radical Pierre-Joseph Proudhon (1809–1865), taking up an argument put by his countryman Jean-Jacques Rousseau (*see 4:476*). Much egalitarian thought was inspired by a religious belief that all men, being equal in the sight of God, should share equally in the world's riches.

An early-twentieth-century postcard shows the ideal village of Bournville, built by English chocolate makers to house the staff of their factory.

The American Situation

In America, people with aims like those of Europe's liberals came under the banner of Jacksonian democracy, because many pinned their hopes on Andrew Jackson, president from 1829 to 1837 (*see 5:650*). The American experience was different from the European. The United States had cast off monarchy and, at least, claimed universal male suffrage. The opening of the West provided a safety valve: discontented workers could emigrate, helping the nation avoid the worst excesses of urban deprivation. Jacksonian democracy was essentially a protest by agricultural states in the South and West against the domination of government by the commercial interests of the East. The West was also home to two reforming movements later in the century. Populism grew out of farmers' alliances in

This pamphlet was issued in Austria to celebrate May Day in 1901. The May Day holiday—traditionally a time for celebrating the arrival of spring—was designated an international labor day by the Second International in 1889.

The Birth of Communism

In *The Communist Manifesto*, published in 1848, Karl Marx and Friedrich Engels formulated theories that would have a profound philosophical and political effect on the world. Although communism came to be seen in the twentieth century as an enemy of individual freedom, liberal thought, and capitalist economics, its roots lay in a vision of an ideal world for everyone. Marx's theory belongs in a tradition of so-called utopian thought that imagines a perfect world of equality, free from either private property or national states.

Marx (1818–1883) and Engels (1820–1895) were both German scholars who spent much of their lives living in England. Engels, who had lived for some years in Manchester, where he later became a successful owner of a cotton mill, had already written a book exposing the housing and working conditions endured by the workers in the textile factories of northern England. He and Marx came to the conclusion that, if things were to get better, the working classes, or proletariat, needed to act together wherever industry was expanding. They would overthrow the existing ruling powers and establish government by the proletariat.

Marx himself called his brand of socialism not communism but "scientific socialism." In his massive work, *Das Kapital*, he attempted to create a universal theory to explain human society. Part of Marx's inspiration came from the work of Charles Darwin, who had accounted for the development of natural history with his theory of evolution (*see 5:698*).

Marx based his theory on his understanding of history, from which he argued that economic laws governed social development. The basic law was that all history was the story of classes at war against each other. There were three such classes: the aristocracy, or landowners; the bourgeoisie, who were middle-class merchants, bankers, factory owners, and traders; and the proletariat, the workers who sell their labor to make industrial products with their own hands.

In Marx's view, every society would pass from the dominance of the aristocracy to that of the bourgeoisie. Marx saw this transition in the English revolution of the seventeenth century and the French Revolution of the eighteenth century (*see 2:235 and 5:583*). Next, the workers would rise up to replace the middle class. Eventually, classes would simply wither away, and the socialist heaven would emerge where everyone gave according to his or her abilities and everyone received according to his or her needs.

While Marx's analysis of history remains generally accepted by historians, his forecast for the future proved far more controversial and less convincing. He believed that the rise of the workers was inevitable, although he also urged them into action to make it happen. The last sentences of the Communist Manifesto ended with a rallying call printed in capital letters: "The proletarians have nothing to lose but their chains. They have a world to win. WORKING MEN OF ALL COUNTRIES, UNITE!"

Friederich Engels, though he is usually seen as Marx's junior partner in the formulation of communist thought, actually had more practical experience of workers' lives than his more famous colleague.

The Communist Manifesto inspired some revolutionary activity in mid-nineteenth-century Europe, but its authors spent a decade in political isolation. Marx was desperately poor: his family lived on bread and potatoes, hiding from debt collectors.

In 1864, Marx emerged from isolation to inspire the First International. In 1871, after his support of a short-lived Paris workers' government called the Paris Commune, Marx became a symbol of workers' revolution. He also became a target for the ruling classes, calling himself the most hated and most threatened man in London.

Marx's work proved highly influential. In the twentieth century, communism dominated the political thinking of Soviet Russia and other countries, such as Fidel Castro's Cuba. Marxism has been partly discredited by the totalitarian nature of many Marxist states, yet Marx's vision remains a powerful one. The epitaph on his tomb reads: "Philosophers have so far explained the world in various ways: the point, however, is to change it."

This statue of Karl Marx stood in the center of Moscow. The dictatorial character of a leader such as Stalin eventually discredited many of Marx's ideas, yet the thinker remains highly respected for his analysis of human history.

Translations of *The Communist Manifesto* in various languages, including Russian and Chinese. The *Manifesto* remains one of the most influential books ever written.

The U.S. artist Victor Gatto painted this image of the Triangle Shirtwaist Company fire around 1911. Fire truck ladders could only reach to the sixth floor, leaving many people trapped by flames on the upper stories of the building.

the 1890s. It aimed at achieving economic parity for agriculture with other businesses and proposed a system of direct election to the Senate. Progressivism had similar aims. Both movements were soon subsumed into the Democratic Party.

In Europe, especially in Great Britain, a burst of reforms in the 1830s and 1840s dealt with the problems of industrializa-

tion. New laws prevented child labor in the mines and limited the hours men and women could work. The first public health act was passed in 1848, partly as a response to outbreaks of cholera. As more Europeans worked in factories, other countries followed Britain's lead. By 1914, virtually every European nation had a code of labor legislation. In the United States, cam-

A striking laborer sits outside his shantytown home during the Pullman Strike of 1894. The strike against the Pullman company by the American Railroad Union spread to twenty-seven states before the U.S. government sent in federal troops after two months to end the dispute. The strike demonstrated the government's determination to apply antitrust laws against labor unions, severely weakening labor's ability to take strike action.

paigners such as the photographer Lewis Wickes Hine (1874–1940) surveyed the miseries of child workers.

In March 1911, a fire at the New York City Triangle Shirtwaist Company killed 146 sweatshop workers, most of them very young immigrant girls. Workers trapped on the top floors of the building were locked in by their employers to prevent theft. So many people were crammed into the sweatshop that the fire escape collapsed under those trying to escape. The disaster led to the introduction of legislation to regulate health and safety at work, including fire codes and laws against child labor.

The Internationals

In Europe, Karl Marx was one of a group of socialists who banded together to found an international movement dedicated to overthrowing capitalism and installing a socialist society in its place. The First International Workingmen's Association was established at a meeting in London in 1864. Marx delivered the opening address and became the first president of what became known as the International. Annual meetings were held in various cities. In 1871, Frenchman Eugène Pottier wrote the *Internationale*, which became the anthem of the movement.

From the beginning, however, the International was split. A quarrel raged between socialists and anarchists, led by the Russian Mikhail Bakunin (1814–1876). Anarchists hated the state, because they objected to all power that was not collectively exercised by all the people in a

Anarchisten-Auslieferung wäre nicht ohne!
Damit wäre dem Czaren, Onkel Sam, am meisten aber dem ehrlichen Arbeiter in Amerika geholfen.

community. "All exercise of power perverts and all submission to authority humiliates," Bakunin wrote. The anarchists wished to destroy the state; Marx's followers, on the other hand, saw the state as a necessary evil that would be the instrument by which the proletariat overthrew the

A cartoon from the early twentieth century shows Uncle Sam kicking an anarchist out of America into Russia. The American government was alarmed by potentially threatening anarchist activity in support of workers' rights.

An electoral poster for the 1904 presidential election shows Socialist Party candidate Eugene V. Debs and his running mate, Ben Hanford. Debs ran for president a total of five times between 1900 and 1920.

815

Shown in a typically combative pose, Jean Jaurès (1859–1914) was the leading French socialist in the years before World War I. When he tried to keep workers out of the coming conflict, which he saw as a capitalist war, he was assassinated.

an empress of Austria, a king of Italy, and a president of the United States, William McKinley, who was shot dead in 1901. Such assassinations achieved nothing, however; the Marxists dismissed them as empty romantic flourishes.

The Second International lasted until 1914. By then, socialist parties were represented in most European parliaments. The Independent Labour Party was founded in Great Britain in 1893. In Germany, the Social Democrats had risen to become the largest party in parliament. Even in the United States, where socialism struggled to make headway against a tradition of individualistic self reliance, Eugene V. Debs (1855–1926) won nearly a million votes as the Socialist candidate in the 1920 presidential election, despite then being in jail for criticizing the government.

World War I

The outbreak of World War I marked the undoing of the high hopes that the first generation of socialists had of building an international workers' brotherhood. Europe's national parliaments were asked to vote their governments money to fight the war. The International called on all socialists in those parliaments to vote against their capitalist governments and refuse to give them the money they needed. Despite the opposition to the coming conflict of leading radical thinkers, such as Jean Jaurès in France, only two European deputies voted against the war, in Serbia. The rest placed patriotism before international socialism.

The International was a spent force, but radicals could take pride in their progress through the century. In 1800, Europe had been ruled by elite minorities with little interest in the general welfare of the people. By 1914, almost every country had universal male suffrage, although only in New Zealand and Finland were women allowed to vote. The most advanced industrial countries, including the United States, had come to accept that government had to intervene in economic affairs to provide for the mass of the people. Governments made provision for unemployment insurance, for instance, and regulated health and safety at work.

Socialism was far from dead. The war that marked the end of one socialist dream would also mark the beginning of another. In 1917, discontent with the war contributed to the outbreak of revolution in Russia (*see 7:909*). For Marxists and other radicals, the chance had come to put their communist experiment into practice.

bourgeoisie. The split between the two groups became so bitter that Bakunin was expelled from the International in 1872. Four years later, at Philadelphia, the International was dissolved.

The Second International

A Second International was founded in 1889, but the old argument continued. In the last years of the century, the anarchists came to rely more and more on the weapon of assassination. They had a record of success. Their most important victims included a Russian czar, a French president,

Correctly dressed for Europe even in the heart of Africa, two European missionaries pose with their African porters in this photograph taken around 1900.

The Scramble for Africa

Europeans Partition the Continent

By 1800, Europeans had explored much of the globe, with the exception of remote areas such as Australia and Antarctica. Although Europeans had long traded with what they called the "Dark Continent," surprisingly they knew nothing about its interior. In twenty years before 1900, however, European powers divided up virtually the whole continent in what was called the scramble for Africa.

European exploration had overlooked the African interior for numerous reasons. The tropical climate and diseases, such as malaria, were often fatal for Europeans. Attempts at expansion met resistance from well-established African societies. Above all, Europeans had little need to venture beyond the coast. Their interest in Africa was limited to trade. The continent provided ivory, gold dust, cocoa, and above all, slaves (*see 3:375*).

Arabs from the north and east had long carried on a trade in slaves. Since the sixteenth century, moreover, some twelve to fifteen million black Africans had been transported as slaves to the New World,

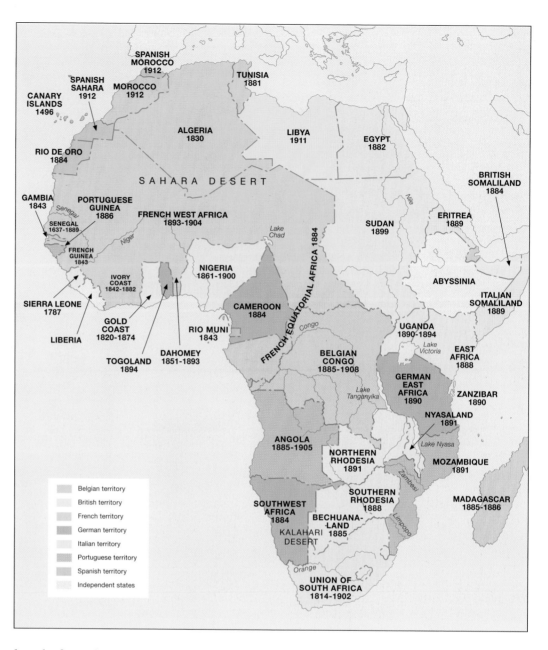

This map shows the political divisions of Africa established by European powers by around 1900.

largely from the southern seaboard of the bulge of West Africa, the Slave Coast. Slavers waited in forts on the relatively healthy coasts for African intermediaries to deliver slaves from the interior. Europe's footholds in Africa reflected the trade. British, French, Dutch, and Portuguese forts dotted the west coast but were rarer in the east. At the tip of the continent stood Cape Colony, a Dutch settlement intended to supply ships bound for Asia (*see 3:328*).

Africa in 1800

Africa had witnessed the rise and fall of civilizations for centuries (*see 1:109*). The states of North Africa were bound by trade and the Islamic faith to the Arab world and by geography and history to the Mediterranean and beyond. Egypt, for example, was part of a Turkish empire that stretched into central Europe (*see 6:727*). In central Africa, below the Sahara Desert and the

Sudan, urban peoples flourished in walled towns amid the plains and forests of west Africa and the Congo Basin. Europeans marveled at Benin, in modern Nigeria, as large as most cities on their own continent.

Towns and villages of northern and central Africa were bound by complex trade networks. Caravans from Morocco, Algeria, and Egypt carried slaves and gold dust from the trading cities of central Africa to port cities, such as Cairo. Seaborne traders connected Africa's east coast to a network that stretched across the Indian Ocean (*see 1:112*). With Arabian trade came Arabian ideas: the Islamic faith had spread through the Sudan to Africa's east coast and the forests of the west.

The Zulu and the Mfecane

Southern Africa comprised narrow coastal plains and grassy or bush-covered uplands. This was the home of the Bantu peoples, cattle-breeding pastoralists who grazed their animals on the coastal plains. Their traditional way of life was threatened by the Dutch settlement at the Cape, which blocked their expansion. Meanwhile, the Zulu, a small Bantu clan from Natal, began a process of imperial expansion.

That expansion was led by Shaka Zulu (c. 1787–1828), a warrior once banished from the tribe because his parents had broken a taboo on intermarrying. Brought up by a neighboring people, Shaka returned to rule the Zulu with an iron hand, killing anyone who opposed him. Shaka reorganized the army into disciplined regiments that he trained to use devastating new tactics and weapons. Shaka attacked his smaller neighbors, incorporating defeated peoples into the Zulu, whose numbers increased fourfold in one year. In 1818, Shaka became king of the Zulu. Before his death ten years later, his constant wars had left modern Natal devastated and empty.

The Zulu expansion had a cumulative effect throughout southern Africa. The ripples of this Mfecane, or "crushing," spread as clans displaced by the Zulu searched for new lands. They moved south to the Cape, across the Transvaal, and into what is now western Zambia. Some became increasingly militaristic, fighting other clans for land; others formed alliances to resist the Zulu, as in Swaziland.

European Incursions

Europe's attitude toward Africa began to change in the early nineteenth century as the slave trade declined. Europeans were becoming less comfortable with the idea of slavery, particularly as plantation owners from the New World began to bring their slaves home to Europe. A problem that had been out of sight was now too close to home for many of Europe's Christians. In 1787, a group of British philanthropists founded the colony of Sierra Leone in West Africa to provide a home for freed slaves. In 1807, after campaigning by evangelical Christians and Quakers, Britain banned the slave trade, as did the United States in 1808 and the Netherlands in 1814. Twenty-five years later, Britain banned slavery itself. Most European states followed suit. The United States abolished the practice in 1865 after the Civil War (*see 5:682*). In 1888, the abolition of slavery in Brazil marked the end of the Atlantic slave trade.

To enforce the ban on the slave trade, Britain occupied forts and naval bases on Africa's west coast, searching ships for contraband slaves. The British attempted to substitute legal trading for slavery; the

French did likewise in Senegal, where their political control extended inland some 300 miles (480 km) up the Senegal River.

African farmers were quick to see the advantage in trading with Europe and rushed to grow peanuts, palms, and cocoa for export. Vegetable oils provided lubricants for European industry. From the 1860s, fast steamships carried the goods north. Meanwhile, however, African farmers neglected to grow essential food crops, while silt from deforested hills clogged rivers and caused flooding.

Adventurers and Missionaries

Trade was only one stimulus to European exploration. Africa attracted a host of individuals with the promise of wealth, adventure, or the chance to spread the Christian message. At the end of the eighteenth century, wealthy Englishmen formed the Association for the Discovery of the Interior

This 1847 painting by a European artist shows a Zulu warrior in ceremonial attire. The Zulu use of the short assegai, a spear used for stabbing at close quarters, was far more effective than the traditional means of fighting by throwing long, thin spears at the enemy.

819

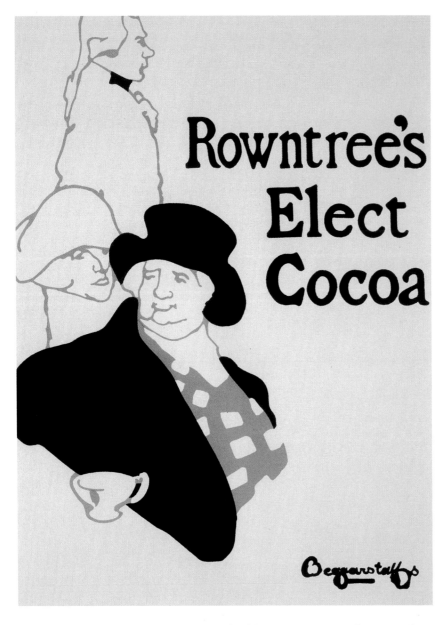

Rowntree's Elect Cocoa

Beggarstaffs

This nineteenth-century poster advertises cocoa powder for making chocolate drinks. The export of cocoa from Africa began early in the century, supplementing the supply from South America and making chocolate more readily available in Europe.

Parts of Africa to sponsor explorers such as Mungo Park, who explored the Niger River. After the explorers came botanists, cartographers, and a host of others eager to discover what Africa had to offer.

For Protestant and Catholic missionaries, Africa was a continent in need of redemption. For much of the century, missionary activity was the preserve of individuals such as the Scot David Livingstone (1813–1873). Livingstone was as much explorer as missionary, traveling north from the Cape into central East Africa in the 1850s. Livingstone, like many other Europeans, saw Africa's native population as needing to be freed from ignorance, famine, and disease. Such thinking was encouraged later in the century by Social Darwinism, a theory that argued that some races were naturally superior to others (see 5:601).

Livingstone's travels stimulated European interest in Africa. A young Welsh war correspondent, Henry Morton Stanley

(1841–1904), was sent by his newspaper proprietor to find the missionary in Africa. Stanley's words on finding the Scotsman after an arduous journey—"Dr. Livingstone, I presume?"—were seen as the epitome of understatement. They made him famous.

Like Livingstone, Stanley spent a lifetime exploring Africa. Like Livingstone, too, Stanley believed that commerce would be decisive in "civilizing" the continent. Returning from an expedition to the Congo Basin, Stanley met with envoys from the Belgian king, Leopold I, who was eager to learn what commercial opportunities the area offered. Exploration was about to become intimately linked with empire.

Northern Africa

European imperialism in Africa had an unpromising beginning. Napoleon's efforts to make Egypt part of his empire had been thwarted by Britain (see 5:596). The Egyptians, led by Muhammad Ali, now claimed independence from the declining Ottoman Empire (see 6:732). In 1830, partly to rally support at home for King Charles X, a French force occupied Algiers, in modern Algeria, supposedly to combat Arab piracy in the Mediterranean. The venture failed to save the king, who was overthrown in the July Revolution (see 5:608), but it left a lasting French presence in northern Africa. In 1832, Arab and Berber tribes from the Algerian interior launched a jihad, or holy war, against the invaders. French troops drove the rebels inland, toward the deserts of North Africa. By 1881, the French had cleared the coastal area and established a protectorate over neighboring Tunisia.

Unlike the earlier colonization of America, in which European disease and aggression effectively wiped out many native peoples (see 3:390), the incursion into Africa usually involved displacing native inhabitants rather than exterminating them. North Africa's Muslim peoples, in any case, would prove more resilient than the Aztecs or North Americans, reemerging in the twentieth century to throw off colonial rule.

Meanwhile, the French public questioned the value of the African venture. The campaign cost the lives of perhaps 150,000 soldiers and almost as many civilians. French settlers proved somewhat reluctant to colonize Algeria, though some did move into the cities, where they were joined by Italian, Spanish, and Maltese settlers.

Southern Africa

The Dutch settlers of the Cape had evolved into the hardy Boers, a Dutch word for farmers, who clashed with their masters, the

The Zambesi River tumbles over Victoria Falls in this photograph. In 1855 David Livingstone became the first European to see the waterfall, which the Africans called "the smoke that thunders."

Dutch East India Company. Many Boers drifted into the interior, away from company control. Transfer of the Cape Colony to British control in the Napoleonic Wars of 1793 to 1815 hastened the Boer movement across the high veld and into southern Natal. Strict Calvinists, the Boers saw themselves as divinely appointed to rule the wilderness and its inhabitants. In the Great Trek of 1835 to 1843, some 12,000 of the migrant farmers moved into land left relatively empty by the Mfecane. They eventually clashed with the Zulu in Natal, which the Boers proclaimed a republic in 1839.

When the British annexed Natal, the Boers moved on again, eventually settling in two regions, the South African Republic, or Transvaal, and the Orange Free State. The British recognized the colonies, and both they and the Boers committed themselves to a policy of apartheid, the strict separation of whites and blacks.

European expansion brought upheaval to native peoples already disturbed by the Mfecane. The British fought a series of wars against the Xhosa, gradually annexing their territory. In 1857, following a prophecy that promised a miraculous victory over the British, the Xhosa slaughtered all their cattle and killed their crops. In the ensuing famine, some 20,000 to 30,000 Xhosa died; an equal number moved to Cape Colony to search for work. Xhosa resistance to the British reappeared only in 1877. That same year, claiming to be protecting the Boers from the Zulu, Britain annexed the Transvaal, but found themselves fighting both the Zulu and the Boers. The British reversed their policy in 1881.

The Changing Nature of Colonialism
European involvement in Africa was by 1880 still largely limited to ill-defined trading zones that caused little competition at home. In 1869, Britain and France cooperated to build the Suez Canal in Egypt. The 92-mile (150 km) canal joined the Mediterranean to the Red Sea, doing away with the long sea voyage around Africa to reach Asia from Europe. France and Britain established a joint protectorate over Egypt to guarantee their investment.

This statue of David Livingstone stands near Victoria Falls, which he named in honor of the British queen. Livingstone once declared, "I shall strike a path into the interior, or perish."

821

French foreign legionaries seize tribesmen's sheep for food during the 1880s in this European print. The legion was formed in 1831 to help control France's African holdings.

belief in the superiority of one's own nation, went hand in hand with the belief that other cultures were inferior.

The Congo and the Berlin Conference

Chancellor Otto von Bismarck, who masterminded the unification of Germany, was Europe's dominant politician. He skillfully exploited colonial rivalry for Germany's domestic advantage. By encouraging other countries' colonial ventures, he could divert tension from Europe—particularly between France and Germany—or create threats to the balance of power in order to reinforce or alter the system of alliances between Europe's leading states. Bismarck's most decisive interference came with the Berlin Conference of 1885.

In 1876, King Leopold of Belgium (1835–1909) had founded the International Association of the Congo. Using the explorer Stanley to make deals with some 450 local chiefs, Leopold made a vast area of central Africa a virtual private estate. Belgian overseers used natives as forced labor

The seeds of European competition in Africa had been sown, however. The continent was assuming a greater importance in European affairs. It provided a new market for finished goods, as Britain's industrial primacy was equaled by other nations and protectionist duties closed Europe's markets (*see 5:621*). Africa also supplied raw materials to sustain industrialization and offered rich returns for investors. The economic impulse behind imperialism was not always simple. France was less industrialized than Belgium, for example, yet sought more colonies. Sweden, whose trading fleet was second in size only to that of Britain, did not seek African colonies at all.

Historical, political, and strategic causes also shaped European attitudes. The unification of Italy and, particularly, Germany upset Europe's balance of power (*see 5:655*). Competition between European states spread around the world, as none could afford to allow the others any strategic advantage. European nationalism, the

to build a railroad and to collect rubber, palm oil, and ivory. Punishments such as whipping, execution, and mutilation ensured that laborers met their work quotas. In some thirty years of Belgian rule, the population of the Congo would suffer a drastic decline.

When Britain and Portugal prepared to challenge Leopold's ambitions in 1885, Bismarck called a conference of European powers at Berlin. The conference agreed that Leopold should keep his territory, although the Congo and Niger Rivers were to remain open to all shipping. More significantly, the conference ruled that any power that established a presence in Africa and informed the other powers thus established a claim to an exclusive "sphere of influence."

The conference effectively began a scramble as European powers rushed to establish themselves in Africa. The British and French led the way, with the new states of Germany and Italy following. For Portugal and Spain, long-disregarded African footholds such as Angola, Mozambique, and the Spanish Sahara once again became valuable.

The scramble introduced a new kind of imperialism. Only a handful of European administrators might effectively claim a territory without exploring it or going near disputed borders. Most decisions on the limits of influence were made in European palaces and offices, often by drawing boundaries on inaccurate maps.

When Europeans did seek to turn lines on a map into a physical presence, they had an increasing number of advantages. The discovery of quinine lifted the barrier of malaria. Motorboats, modern rifles, and machine guns made it possible for small groups of Europeans to overcome larger native armies armed with hand weapons.

The French in the Sudan

The French hold on the Senegal River in West Africa convinced them that they might gain control of the Sudan. The plains of the Sudan lay between the Sahara to the north and the rain forests of central Africa

Crowds line the banks to watch the opening procession of ships on the Suez Canal in November 1869 in this contemporary print. The canal cut the journey time from Europe to Asia from three months to three weeks.

823

The Appeal of Empire

The French Romantic artist Eugène Delacroix painted this Moroccan soldier in 1845. Delacroix was fascinated by the culture of northern Africa.

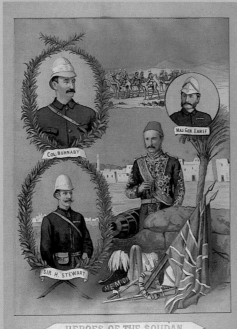

This typical example of a late-nineteenth-century patriotic print is entitled *Heroes of the Soudan*, or Sudan. It shows British military leaders including, in the middle, General Gordon.

The desire to acquire empires that gripped many European countries during the nineteenth century had many causes. Some were practical, such as the belief that colonies would benefit trade or would be of strategic or military use. Others lay deeper within human nature, touching on religion, morality, and ideas of superiority. Some Europeans argued that Christians were obliged to spread God's word to non-Christian peoples or that they had a duty to introduce all people to a better, more civilized way of life. Others argued simply that it is the nature of individuals and states to try to dominate others. This argument was boosted both by nationalistic beliefs that rated one people superior to another and by Social Darwinism, which argued that, in society as in nature, the strong would dominate the weak.

Another argument for imperialism was that it enhanced a nation's prestige. In the twentieth century, the Italian dictator Mussolini set out to emulate the great days of the ancient Roman Empire. Significantly, he began by conquering Abyssinia, the home of the Ethiopians who defeated the Italians in 1896.

Imperialism in Africa was particularly attractive to Europeans. They called Africa the Dark Continent and imagined it to be full of untamed jungles, burning deserts, and savage inhabitants. When David Livingstone visited England in 1856 to lecture, audiences listened in awe to his descriptions of a pleasant land of fruit orchards and shady groves.

For Europeans, Africa conjured up images of adventure and heroism. It was a land where individuals, usually if not always male, could distinguish themselves with feats of courage and daring. Explorers such as the French count Pierre Savorgnan de Brazza in the Congo and the German Gerhard Rohlfs, who explored the Sahara Desert, caught the public imagination. Soldiers such as Britain's General Charles G. Gordon became heroes. Gordon, who died in Sudan, was already famed as Chinese Gordon for his role in protecting European interests during China's Taiping Rebellion (*see 6:771*).

Africa was exotic, too. The nineteenth century saw the Arab countries of northern Africa win their enduring reputation for romance. African culture fascinated European artists and composers in the same way as they were fascinated by the art of China and Japan (*see 6:784*). In the early twentieth century, artists such as Modigliani and Picasso introduced new forms of painting to Europe, inspired by African carving.

to the south. Long fabled as one of the continent's richest regions, the Sudan tempted the French across Africa. Although the French public was traditionally anti-imperial, a handful of glory-seeking army officers were swayed by the dream of a vast triangular African empire connecting the Atlantic, the Mediterranean, and the Indian Ocean.

The British, meanwhile, claimed Sudan, a region east of the Sudan plains and south of Egypt. Nationalist uprisings had given the British troops the opportunity to enter Egypt in 1881, ostensibly to protect the Suez Canal, and take control of the country. While the French dreamed of an empire stretching across Africa, British imperialists aspired to build a railroad that joined the Cape to Cairo, bringing the length of the continent under British control.

War in the Sudan

In theory, control of Egypt gave the British control of Sudan: they established an Anglo-Egyptian protectorate over the area. In effect, nobody controlled the vast region. The British were driven out in 1885 by the Sudanese religious leader, the Mahdi, at the cost of the life of the British hero General Charles G. Gordon.

As the French advanced from the west, their opportunity to find a gap between British spheres of influence came at Fashoda, a ruined fortress lying between Anglo-Egyptian Sudan to the north and British Uganda to the south. In 1898, after a year's march, a small French force reached Fashoda only a fortnight before a superior British force arrived from Sudan. A standoff ensued in the desert, while the media in both countries roused the public into a mood of warlike nationalism. Their governments were more realistic, however. Britain's naval dominance of the Mediterranean gave the French little choice but to give up the fort. In return, the British agreed not to challenge French territorial claims elsewhere in Africa.

Meanwhile, other European powers rushed to fill the gaps still left in Africa. The Germans seized Togoland, Cameroon, German Southwest Africa, and German East Africa. Italy claimed Libya, Italian Somaliland, and Eritrea.

Control and Resistance

The ease with which European powers took control of their African claims varied greatly. At the Battle of Omdurman in Sudan in 1898, a British army led by Lord

A contemporary lithograph shows the Battle of Omdurman on September 2, 1898. The British redcoats used rifle and machine-gun fire to repel the attacks of the far larger forces of the Mahdi, Sudan's religious leader.

825

This cartoon of 1892 shows Cecil Rhodes standing astride Africa, with one foot in Cairo, the other in Cape Town. Rhodes, who originally traveled to southern Africa seeking a warm climate to combat ill health, became a symbol of British imperial aggression in Africa.

THE RHODES COLOSSUS

STRIDING FROM CAPE TOWN TO CAIRO.

Black workers set out from Cape Colony for the goldfields at Witwatersrand in 1886. Gold drew many prospectors to the Transvaal, encouraging the British to believe that they could destabilize the colony.

Kitchener decisively defeated the army of the Mahdi at the cost of fewer than thirty dead. Greater numbers of African troops also overcame European forces, however, as when some 20,000 Zulu warriors over-whelmed a British and native force of 1,300 in 1879 at Ishandhlwana. On some rare occasions, African forces enjoyed the same weaponry as their opponents. In 1896 at Adowa, Menelik II of Ethiopia, who had equipped his army with the latest firearms, defeated an Italian army in a straight fight. Italy's defeat guaranteed that, by the time World War I broke out in 1914, Ethiopia was one of the few African regions not occupied by European powers.

South Africa

The biggest challenge to British imperial expansion came in southern Africa, where the British faced opposition not only from Africans such as the Zulu but also from the Boers. The stability of the region was upset in 1886, when gold was discovered in Witwatersrand in the Boer Transvaal. Within a decade, the colony was producing one-fifth of the world's gold, at a time when gold was increasingly important to support monetary systems. The British effectively hired the mining magnate Cecil Rhodes (1853–1902) to win control of the goldfields.

As director of the British South Africa Company, Rhodes had already led British expansion north from the Cape into Bechuanaland and what later became Rhodesia. He was a passionate supporter of British imperialism, once declaring: "If there be a God, I think what he would like me to do is to paint as much of Africa British-red as possible." In late 1895, Rhodes authorized a raid by his assistant, Dr. Starr Jameson, into the Transvaal, in a failed attempt to inspire an armed uprising by *uitlanders*, or non-Boer citizens, against the government.

The Germans, sensing a chance to humiliate Britain, congratulated the Boer president, Paul Kruger (1825–1904), on resisting the raid and supplied arms to the Boers. It was typical of the complex relation between imperialism and European politics that, at the same time, the Germans were trying unsuccessfully to force the British into an alliance with them in Europe.

The Boer War

In October 1899, tension between the Boers and the British spilled into war when the Boers invaded British territory. The British defenders were ill prepared and the Boers were able to besiege the towns of Ladysmith, Mafeking, and Kimberley. Reinforcements eventually brought the British military presence to 500,000, however, against a total of some 88,000 Boers. British victory was virtually inevitable, but the Boers' commando tactics inflicted a number of defeats on their enemies before

they finally capitulated in 1902. The British destroyed both Boer and African farms, herding Boer civilian families into unhygienic, ill-supplied concentration camps, where some 28,000 people died, causing international outrage.

Victory left the British dominant in Africa. While the Cairo-to-Cape Town railroad remained a dream, 32,000 Indian workers built a railroad to link British Angola to the east coast. Similar developments in other colonies fostered agriculture and commerce. Apart from the mineral-rich Cape, however, African colonies rarely proved as lucrative as their masters hoped. In a famous phrase, the British writer Rudyard Kipling described Africa not as a source of wealth but as "the white man's burden."

The Black Africans

Haphazard, ineffectual, and unrewarding as it sometimes proved, European control in Africa had profound implications for black Africans. A poet wrote: "A sun of disaster has risen in the West. The Christian calamity has come upon us like a dust cloud." A few Africans grew rich from trade. Others saw their traditional way of life destroyed, from the Congoese forced to labor in Leopold's vast colony to the slave-trading people of the east coast, whose trade was now forbidden. Warfare decimated the Zulu. Britain's conquest of Sudan cost 20,000 native lives.

Continuing resistance to European rule brought more suffering to African peoples. When the Herero people rebelled against German rule in Southwest Africa in 1907, the Germans hanged thousands of them, coordinating the exercise by telegraph. More Hereros were driven into the Kalahari Desert, where they died of starvation or thirst. The population fell from 80,000 to only 15,000, many of whom were in exile. In West Africa, meanwhile, campaigns by the British against the Ashanti and the French against the Mande had less devastating but still highly significant impacts.

Hundreds of thousands of Africans lost their traditional lands and were moved to

A group of Boer commandos show off their German-made Mauser rifles during the Boer War. Despite their numerical inferiority, the Boers' effective use of guerrilla tactics allowed them to inflict a number of defeats on the British forces.

In the heart of British Central Africa, a solitary magistrate holds a court session in this photograph from the 1890s. Colonial powers often tried to re-create their own institutions and standards in Africa, helping confirm the misleading myth that the continent lacked any social organization before the Europeans arrived.

reserves, where the able-bodied were enlisted for arduous work. Some resisted this humiliation, however, living as peasants or migrant workers, thus keeping some control over their own labor. Meanwhile, in South Africa, as the Cape Colony was renamed after the British incorporated the Boer republics, even black Africans who had fought with the British in the Boer War were forbidden from owning land in the most desirable nine-tenths of the country.

Life in the Colonies

For the most part, European governments had few plans for colonies they acquired. The overriding aim was to make colonies self-supporting through trade and taxation so that they would not be a drain on the home country. Profit dominated all other considerations. In central Africa, for example, overlords forced farmers to grow cotton on land normally used to grow food.

Most colonial powers ruled their domains in similar ways, using a governor and district officers who often used local tribal chiefs to put policies into practice. Where a colonial power was weak, African uprisings remained frequent. The Portuguese in Angola and Mozambique conducted mili-

tary campaigns against the population virtually every year from 1875 to 1924 before they subdued all resistance.

In the main, colonial powers had little interest in improving the lives of their African subjects. Education, for example, was controlled by missionaries, who taught rudimentary reading, writing, and math. Mission schools were one of the few ways for black Africans to improve their lot.

Such elementary education nevertheless helped some of the Africans who began to form anticolonial movements, whose heyday would come after World War I (*see 8:1117*). In southern Africa, inspiration came from an Indian lawyer working in the Cape Colony. Shocked by the racism he witnessed, Mohandas Gandhi, later known as Mahatma Gandhi (1869–1948), launched the South African Indian Congress to seek rights for Indians (*see 8:1107*). An organization for African rights, the South African Native National Congress, was formed in 1912. Five years later, it took the name by which it is still known, the African National Congress, or ANC. Such movements would grow stronger and more widespread throughout the century, eventually returning all of Africa to African control (*see 9:1221*).

The Triumph of the Dollar

Recovery and Prosperity in the United States

The end of the Civil War in 1865 left the United States devastated and divided. By the end of the century, however, rapid industrialization had made the country the dominant economy in the world. Settlers pushed the frontier west to claim the whole continent for the United States, displacing the Native American inhabitants of the land, while an aggressive foreign policy confirmed U.S. primacy over its neighbors.

The Years of Reconstruction

At the end of the Civil War, the victors faced the problem of how to treat the South. Some wanted to impose harsh punishment on their enemies. These radical politicians believed that the war had been fought not only to preserve the Union but to guarantee freedom and principles that should now be forced on the South, particularly with relation to the region's 4.5 million black citizens. This policy of changing southern society was called Reconstruction. Other Unionists sought to

reintegrate the rebel states into the Union through a more lenient approach. President Abraham Lincoln (1809–1865) offered the best chance for moderating the two opinions. On April 14, 1865, however, he was assassinated in a theater by the southern sympathizer John Wilkes Booth.

Lincoln's successor was his vice president Andrew Johnson (1808–1875), a southern Democrat who had remained loyal to the Union. Lincoln's Republican Party supported Johnson until it became clear that he would not impose the will of the North on the South. He argued that the government had only limited power to force states to act in a certain way. Johnson pardoned former Confederate leaders and allowed them again to participate in state government. Johnson also left it to those governments to decide the future of their black populations. The president made his own position clear: "This is a country for white men and, by God, so long as I am president, it shall be a government for white men."

In *Across the Continent: Westward the Course of Empire Takes Its Way*, painted in 1868, artist Fanny Palmer depicts an imaginary frontier as the railroad opens the Great Plains for settlement. Westward expansion was one of the defining characteristics of the United States in the second half of the nineteenth century.

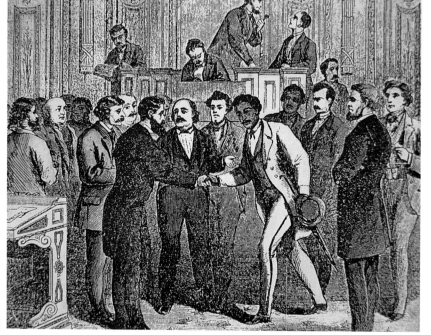

This engraving of 1879 depicts black Americans emigrating from the South to Kansas and St. Louis.

John W. Menard, the first African American congressman, takes his seat in the House of Representatives in December 1868.

The Thirteenth Amendment had abolished slavery after the war, but it had not stopped racial oppression. The state governments sanctioned by Johnson adopted "black codes" that kept freedmen in a state as near to slavery as possible. The abolitionist Frederick Douglass exclaimed: "They were free! Free to hunger, free to the pitiless wrath of enraged masters.... Free, without roofs to cover them, or bread to eat, or land to cultivate."

The black codes enraged Republicans in Congress. They approved the Fourteenth Amendment, which excluded ex-Confederate leaders from politics and granted equality before the law to all citizens, including freed slaves. Another act prolonged the life of the Freedmen's Bureau, a welfare agency set up in March 1865 to help ex-slaves. The president vetoed both acts.

The Republicans won Congressional elections in 1866, and the next year, they passed a Reconstruction Act that placed Southern states under military control and forced them to implement the Fourteenth Amendment. Johnson's continued obstruction of Congress led to his impeachment; he was acquitted in the Senate by one vote. In 1868, he lost the presidency to Ulysses S. Grant, the Union war hero.

The Southern Backlash

By July 1870, all the former Confederate states had been readmitted to the Union. They still refused to treat black Americans as the North wished, however. When the Fifteenth Amendment gave freedmen the right to vote in 1870, threats of violence and pressure from their planter employers

830

kept blacks away from the polls. The threat of violence was very real. In Memphis and New Orleans in 1866, rioting whites attacked and killed African Americans.

Among the chief exponents of terrorism in the South was the Ku Klux Klan. This secret society, founded in 1865 by former Confederate soldiers, was dedicated to preserving white supremacy by violence. Klan members hunted their victims at night and erected burning crosses near their homes. In 1869, the organization's leaders disbanded it for being too violent. The Klan went underground and the government took steps to suppress its activities 1871. It was resurrected in the 1920s and 1950s.

There were many reasons for the South's continued hostility toward the North and toward blacks: the defeat and cost of the war, a belief in white superiority, and the destruction of the southern economy. The abolition of slavery left the cotton economy in ruins because it had been built on forced labor for which planters now had to pay. Whites with land and blacks with nothing but their labor turned to sharecropping. Blacks became tenant farmers on land owned by whites who did not pay them wages but allowed them a share of the value of the crop after deducting the cost of seeds, tools, and rent. A series of bad harvests and an agricultural depression in the 1870s left much of the South bitterly poor.

Southerners directed their bitterness against the administrations that oversaw Reconstruction. These northerners—called carpetbaggers because of the bags in which they carried their belongings—were sometimes opportunist profiteers. Others, however, were often dedicated men and women willing to risk their lives to establish a solid educational and political base in the South, as were their southern allies, called scalawags. Both groups earned little but hatred from the southerners.

The Rise of the New South
The 1876 presidential election was won by the Republican Rutherford B. Hayes in a rigged ballot that earned him nicknames, such as Rutherfraud. The election of the moderate Hayes effectively marked the end of Reconstruction. The energy had gone out of the movement, leaving the South to restore Democratic governments that soon adopted new state laws hostile to southern blacks. In the 1900s, southern states went on to pass Jim Crow laws that segregated the races in services such as schools and hospitals. Black Americans had to wait until the 1960s civil rights movement before these setbacks were reversed.

Reconstruction failed for various reasons. By replacing plantation agriculture with family farms, the government hoped to destroy the South's slaveholding aristocracy. Instead, it created widespread resentment, as did the laws introduced to curb terrorist violence. Had freedmen been given their own land, things might have been different; as it was, Reconstruction depended entirely on the support of southerners, who had little sympathy with its aims. The government abandoned Reconstruction because the North was ultimately more interested in creating a secure environment for investment than protecting black rights.

This illustration from 1868 shows the costumes adopted by the Ku Klux Klan, which had recently emerged to fight measures for racial equality.

831

Workers erect a telegraph line alongside a railroad track in the American West in the 1860s. The spread of the railroad and the telegraph improved communications and helped create a sense of national unity by linking East and West.

Rapid Industrialization

Between the end of the Civil War and 1900, the United States became the world's leading industrial nation. Production increased by 700 percent to double that of Great Britain, the previous leading industrial power. The United States had considerable economic advantages. The expanding West offered raw materials such as timber, coal, oil, and iron. New cities emerged to harness such resources, including the meat-processing center of Chicago, while other cities expanded enormously because of new industry, as Pittsburgh did because of steel manufacture. The United States' other great advantage was the inventiveness of its citizens. Industrial growth encouraged innovation. New inventions ranged from the telegraph to the telephone, from the mechanical reaper to the refrigerated rail-car. Thomas Edison (1847–1931) alone developed the lightbulb, the dynamo, the motion camera, and the gramophone.

Another impulse to growth was the development of trusts. Federal law banned business monopolies, so manufacturers banded together to create trusts, which were monopolies in all but name. This enabled them both to save money by negotiating preferential rates from the railroads or other suppliers and to keep the prices of their goods artificially high. Prominent trusts included the railroad combines, the Standard Oil Company, and the United States Steel Corporation. The people at the top of the trusts, dubbed robber barons by

This patriotic print from 1873, entitled *By Industry We Thrive*, celebrates the dedication and craft of America's industrial workforce.

their opponents for the massive profits they made, dominated the American political and economic system.

The Promised Land

Industrial expansion depended on a supply of cheap, mobile labor. Employers advertised overseas an American dream that offered the chance of prosperity for everyone. Millions of immigrants responded, mainly from the poorer areas of southern and eastern Europe. From 1860 to 1900, the U.S. population rose from 31 million to 76 million. The population of cities such as New York increased fourfold. Immigrants often lived in overcrowded tenement slums where a lack of planned sanitation made health a major problem.

Rapid economic growth outstripped any concern for the welfare of workers. There was no time limit on a working day, for example, as there was throughout most of Europe, and a lack of safety precautions meant that, in the 1890s, some 35,000 workers died each year in industrial accidents. Women and children were used as cheap labor. A labor movement emerged to tackle such problems, but it was ineffective in the face of internal divisions and employers' use of armed force to break strikes.

As industry expanded, the fortunes of America's farmers worsened. Between 1860 and 1890, wheat and cotton prices fell by half, while the cost of transporting the crops rose. Western farmers, finding themselves at the mercy of easterners who ran the railroads and controlled the markets, formed a Farmers' Alliance. The alliance united the South and the West in a call for public ownership of the railroads, a silver-based currency, and shorter working days.

The alliance's early successes at state level led, in 1892, to the formation of the

This photograph from 1896 shows Andrew Carnegie, who became one of the United States' richest men after making a fortune in the steel industry. He was a major charitable benefactor, funding numerous libraries and educational institutions.

This hand-colored photograph from the start of the twentieth century shows an Italian immigrant family arriving at Ellis Island, New York. Between 1892 and 1943, some 17 million immigrants passed through the processing center at Ellis Island, mainly from European countries such as Italy and Ireland.

Populist, or People's, Party. The party represented the first serious challenge to the trusts' monopoly and led to a realignment of the two principal parties. The 1896 elections, held against the background of a financial crash in 1893, brought political tensions to a head. The industrialists threatened economic meltdown if the Populist-aligned Democrats won. Workers voted for their jobs, the Republicans won the election, and the century ended with an economic revival and a new optimism.

American politics at the turn of the century were far more complex than a simple opposition between business interests and social welfare, however. After the upheavals of Reconstruction, the most important characteristic of American democracy was that it was fundamentally healthy. Despite absorbing more than 30 million immigrants from different political cultures in forty years, despite corruption in city government, and despite the disproportionate power of the trusts, Americans were content to express themselves democratically rather than by revolution or civil war.

Although the American economy gave undue influence to a few wealthy men who demanded the freedom to act as they wished and who ruthlessly crushed strikes, those men were often far more complex than was suggested by their robber baron nickname. Andrew Carnegie and John D. Rockefeller were just two of the industrialists who plowed their profits into vast educational and social philanthropy.

Even U.S. attitudes toward peoples such as Hispanic or Native Americans were more complex than the simple displays of racial superiority may sometimes appear. People such as President Theodore Roosevelt (1858–1919), who summed up his attitude to America's neighbors as "speak softly and carry a big stick," were often farsighted social reformers. They believed that Americans had the right to do as they wished but they also believed that, in the long run, this would create a better world for everyone, including even those the United States apparently oppressed.

The Spanish-American War
America's imperial ambitions showed themselves in the 1898 Spanish-American War in Cuba, at around the same time as European nations launched a new burst of imperial rivalry. American investment in Cuba's sugar plantations gave the United States a powerful economic interest in the island. The Monroe Doctrine was used to justify U.S. interference in the affairs of Central and South America.

In 1895, Cuba broke out in revolt against its Spanish rulers. American newspapers campaigned for U.S. intervention in an effort to boost flagging circulation. In 1898, the U.S. battleship *Maine*, in Cuba to protect American interests, exploded in Havana harbor with the loss of 269 lives. The explosion was later found to have been caused by a faulty boiler, but an inquiry at the time blamed Spanish sabotage. President William McKinley (1843–1901) declared war on Spain.

The Americans won an easy victory and occupied Cuba. The peace treaty revealed America's true ambitions. While Cuba became independent, the United States annexed Puerto Rico and Guam and bought the strategically important islands of the Philippines from Spain for $20 million.

Dollar and Big-Stick Diplomacy
Sugar-rich Cuba was not the only target for investment. U.S. money poured into Mexico (*see 6:743*). Costa Rica and other Central American states attracted capital with their fruit industry. Such states were often unstable, however, making investments vulnerable (*see 6:765*). In what became known as dollar diplomacy, the United States sent marines into unstable countries to keep the peace while American officials put their finances in order.

To create the conditions for building the Panama Canal, Theodore Roosevelt, who became president in 1901, encouraged the campaign for Panamanian independence from Colombia and used the U.S. Navy to back the rebels. He declared the United States to be a "police power" on the continent and privately promised to "spank those wretched little republics."

The Panama Canal
The need for a canal connecting the Atlantic to the Pacific was dictated by commercial and strategic reasons. The waterway through the narrowest point of Central America would be a naval link between the Atlantic and Pacific coasts. The French had failed in an earlier attempt to build a similar project. Now, however, the discovery of antidotes to the yellow fever endemic to the region made the scheme practical. After Panama's independence in 1903, the United States guaranteed Panama its protection, along with $10 million and an annual rent, in return for the right to build and manage a canal, which opened in 1914.

Roosevelt the Reformer
Roosevelt was as vigorous at home as he was abroad. Already a hero from the Spanish war, when he had commanded a colorful unit called the Rough Riders, he proved America's most popular leader

This bust of Sitting Bull marks his grave in South Dakota. The Sioux chief fought in the 1876 Battle of the Little Big Horn in which General Custer and his cavalry were all killed. Sitting Bull later joined Buffalo Bill's Wild West Show but remained an agitator for Native American rights.

835

The American artist N. C. Wyeth painted *Covered Wagons* in the early twentieth century. The saillike appearance of the canvas covers earned settlers' wagons the nickname prairie schooners.

since Lincoln. Roosevelt came to power at a time when a wide alliance for reform was emerging in the face of the trusts' relentless pursuit of profit.

America's social problems—grinding poverty and poor working conditions—both gave rise to and were made worse by corruption. William Marcy ("Boss") Tweed of New York was the most notorious of a breed of urban manipulators who formed rings centered on local government through which they controlled the distribution of public contracts, bought off the police, and, either by granting favors or by physical bullying, won the support of large parts of the population at election time.

Roosevelt paid careful attention to public opinion, despite denouncing writers and photographers who campaigned for social improvement as "muckrakers." He responded to disquiet over big business with prosecutions against the trusts that won him a reputation as a trustbuster. In 1902, the president mediated a bitter coal strike in Pennsylvania. The strike led to the creation of a new Cabinet department, Commerce and Labor. In his second

term, Roosevelt passed legislation to regulate the railroads, the meat industry, and food and drug production and to conserve the wilderness in parks such as Yosemite and Yellowstone.

The Progressive Party
In 1908, Roosevelt handed the nomination for president to his Republican colleague William Howard Taft. Four years later, however, Roosevelt returned to lead a wing of the party that called for social reforms, including women's suffrage. The Republicans split, and Roosevelt formed a new Progressive Party. In the 1912 election, Democratic candidate Woodrow Wilson (1856–1924) defeated the divided Republicans. Five years later, he took America into the First World War (*see 7:895*).

The Age of the West
The second half of the nineteenth century was shaped by America's westward expansion. Most Americans supported the philosophy of Manifest Destiny, which gave the United States the moral right–and the moral duty–to expand across the whole of

North America. The first westbound pioneers had crossed the Appalachian Mountains before the American Revolutionary War. Many thousands followed, lured by the promise of gold, fur, and land and the desire for a new way of life. The government encouraged settlers with legislation such as the Homestead Act of 1862, which gave 160 acres of land to anyone willing to cultivate them. Despite this, only an eighth of western land went to farmers. The rest was taken by speculators and the railroads. By 1890, America's frontier reached the Pacific coast and the country was divided into forty-four states.

Many developments in opening up the West were triggered by the 1849 California Gold Rush and later mineral discoveries.

A party of Dutch immigrants pose in front of the train that has carried them to their new homes in Minnesota near the end of the nineteenth century.

An early dressmaker's mannequin still stands in a store window in Bodie, California. Around the 1880s, the flourishing mining town had a population of around 10,000 and a reputation for lawlessness. Today it is a ghost town preserved as a state historic park.

Myth and Reality in the American West

The westward expansion of the United States, particularly after the Civil War, has long exercised a grip on the public imagination. Contemporary artists and writers celebrated the exploits of cowboys and gunfighters, as newspaper proprietors in the East found an eager readership for western, frontier adventures. Throughout Hollywood's history, the Western has remained among the most popular types of movies. To go with the heroic cowboy, the popular mythology of the West required a villain, which it initially supplied in the shape of the Native American,

The qualities that make the West popular are simple: the epic scale of the land, the pioneer's struggle to survive, the adventure, good versus evil in quick-draw life-and-death struggles. This is the story of nation building. For some of its formerly impoverished settlers, the West proved to be the promised land. Most, however, found life no more rewarding there than in the more developed East.

The Hollywood image of the West implies that cowboys and their "wild" world lasted a long time. Their heyday was, in fact, very brief, lasting only from around 1865 to 1885. After the Civil War, Texan cattle owners realized that potentially huge profits could be made by using the railroads to ship cattle to feed the industrial cities of the North and East. Men with good horse-riding skills, often Civil War veterans, were recruited to escort cattle on the 1,500-mile Long Drive from Texas north to railheads in Kansas and Wyoming. Cow towns such as Abilene and Dodge City flourished and became a byword for drunkenness and fighting.

The pattern of settlement in the West soon changed. As settlers arrived on the Great Plains, they used newly invented barbed wire to protect their crops. This limited the open range and brought settlers into conflict with large ranching concerns. The new form of fencing, introduced in 1874, made it far cheaper

A lone cowboy watches a line of cattle in *On the Chisholm Trail*, painted by Frederic Remington in 1872. The works of Remington and other artists were highly popular and did much to shape public perception of the West by depicting the cowboy as a lone hero facing the vastness of nature.

and easier to enclose land than had the previous wooden fences. In Montana, ranchers and settlers clashed in the so-called range wars of the 1880s. The cattle business began to decline under pressure from overstocking and falling demand. The freezing winter of 1886/1887 killed off huge numbers of livestock. The open range eventually became divided into smaller fenced ranches. The cowboy became little more than a picturesque memory, reduced to mending fences.

Another potent stereotype of the mythologized West is the warlike Native American. Native Americans feature in the standard myth as aggressors, attacking settlers' wagon trains, stealing cattle, or surrounding U.S. Army forts. The reality was usually the other way around. Aggression more often than not began with white settlers intruding on Native American territory.

Wherever white settlers arrived in the West, they inevitably disrupted the Native American inhabitants, as Europeans had done since the two peoples first encountered one another in the sixteenth century. European encroachment forced the Native Americans from their traditional lands. Through the Indian Removal Act of 1830, the United States forcibly coerced peoples such as the Cherokee and Seminoles to move west, where they were promised the freedom of the Great Plains.

More and more settlers crossed Native American land, however, particularly after the California Gold Rush of 1848 and 1849 stimulated westward migration and the coming of the railroad encouraged settlement in the Midwest. Thousands of wagon trains crossed the plains, while European hunters slaughtered the buffalo on which Native Americans depended.

The Native Americans hit back with a series of sporadic wars against the U.S. Army that lasted for some thirty years (1862–1890). In 1876, in the famous Battle of the Little Bighorn, Sioux and Cheyenne warriors wiped out a cavalry detachment commanded by General Custer. The next year, Chief Joseph led the Nez Percé against the army, while in the Southwest, Geronimo organized the Chiricahua against the authorities until he was captured and imprisoned in 1888.

In 1890, a religious movement among Native Americans promised the ousting of European settlers, the return of native dead, and the restoration of good health, game animals, and traditional lands. Wovoka (c. 1856–1932), a Paiute prophet, instructed his followers in a new Ghost dance and preached a message of renewal and harmony.

In a short time, the Ghost Dance spread through the plains, reaching the Sioux in 1890. The dance alarmed authorities, who sent the army to suppress it. Sioux leaders of the dance promised Ghost Dancers that their shirts would protect them, but that was not the case. After troops killed their chief, Sitting Bull, a few hundred Sioux surrendered. U.S. troops massacred them in what has been misleadingly described as the Battle of Wounded Knee. The incident marked the end of effective resistance by Native Americans, who henceforth lived primarily on government-allocated reservations.

This photograph taken in 1879 shows Dodge City. The notorious Kansas cattle town stood on the Santa Fe Trail from Texas.

This young girl was photographed working in a Vermont cotton mill in 1910 by the photographer Lewis Hine. Hine campaigned to end child labor in the United States. President Theodore Roosevelt dubbed Hine and other social campaigners "muckrakers."

Around 90,000 people flocked to the West from all over the world. A complete service industry sprang up in their wake as entrepreneurs provided the miners with transport and supplies. The entrepreneurs' profits were more reliable than the chance of striking gold or silver. Both Wells Fargo stagecoaches and the Pony Express began in service to miners in the West. The latter, set up in the early 1860s to run 2,000 miles between Missouri and California, was soon made obsolete by the telegraph.

The Railways

The westward expansion was a story of a large-scale movement of people that only became possible with the coming of the railroads (*see 5:622*). Sponsored by huge government grants, the first transcontinental line was completed in 1869 after a feat of engineering that included crossing the Rockies. The number of miles of track increased from 30,000 to 164,000 in only twenty-five years. The railroads provided the backbone to expansion as new settlements sprang up alongside the tracks. Many of America's most famous engineers started their careers working for the railroads. They included Samuel Morse (1791–1872), who invented the telegraph to prevent the frequent accidents caused by trains running in different directions on the same track.

Conserving the West

The increased settlement of the West caused some alarm among people concerned with the environment. In the 1900s, chief forester Gifford Pinchot persuaded President Roosevelt to support plans for conserving the wilderness. Roosevelt added 150 million acres to the existing 45 million acres of government reserves. These national parks were protected from further exploitation and left in their natural state as a legacy for future generations.

26 Décembre 1888 20 Janvier 1889

The Eiffel Tower rises above Paris in these two photographs taken a month apart during its construction in 1888 and 1889. The completed tower, a triumph of engineering, was adopted by Parisians as a symbol of the excitement and dynamism of their city.

The Arts in the Late Nineteenth Century

New Forms of Expression for New Ways of Life

In the early part of the nineteenth century, the Romantics had turned away from the industrializing world to find consolation in nature and the imagination (*see 5:635*). As the century progressed, the relationship between the increasing pace of industrialization and the arts became more complex. On the one hand, artists became increasingly concerned with the negative effects of industrialization and urbanization. On the other hand, they sought new ways of expression and adopted technological inno-vations, such as the camera. New building materials changed architecture and the appearance of cities. Economic prosperity created an urban workforce with leisure and money to visit art galleries, concert halls, theaters, and museums, resulting in a great expansion of artistic activity.

After around 1850, many artists inter-ested in the modern world tried to depict "real" life rather than self-consciously "beautiful" images. The Frenchman Gustave Courbet (1819–1877) shocked the

This 1860s photograph shows the French poet Charles Baudelaire, a leading influence on modern writing. Echoing developments in the other arts, he rejected the romantic poets for adopting poses and refused to accept that certain subjects were too common or ugly for poetry.

serious art of the Renaissance masters who preceded Raphael (1483–1520) (*see 1:79*). Led by Dante Gabriel Rossetti (1828–1882), the Pre-Raphaelites painted realistically from direct observation, although they often applied the techniques to biblical or legendary scenes. One of them once had to pay doctor's bills after a model caught cold while posing in a bathtub for his picture of a drowning woman.

The Emergence of Photography

One of the most significant changes in the arts came with the invention of the camera. Not only did the camera make creative activity more democratic by allowing anyone to create an image, it also raised profound questions about the nature of painting and perception.

The Frenchman Louis Jacques Daguerre (1789–1851) and the Englishman William Henry Fox Talbot (1800–1877) independently developed techniques to create photographic prints around 1839. Photographic technology developed so rapidly that London had no less than 250 portrait studios by the mid-1860s. That same decade, countless soldiers from the U.S. Civil War posed proudly in their uniforms for souvenir photographs. For the first time, even relatively poor families could afford realistic likenesses of themselves.

The impact on portrait painters was profound. They had fewer commissions, and their clients came increasingly from the upper classes. Where painted portraits were once common among the middle classes, they became a status symbol for the rich. At the end of the century, the American John Singer Sargent (1856–1925) painted almost exclusively portraits of what was known as "society."

Photography and Realism

Photography soon influenced other artists. To some, it offered a useful tool to achieve more realistic effects. In the United States, Eadweard Muybridge took sequences of shots of walking men or galloping horses that showed that people and animals moved very differently from how they were usually portrayed in art. Edgar Degas incorporated the new knowledge in depictions of the racetrack that seem like snapshots in their spontaneity and casual composition. The outstanding American artist Thomas Eakins (1844–1916) based his naturalistic paintings of the human body, often engaged in sports such as rowing, on photographs. The other great American artist of the day, Winslow Homer (1836–1910), made his name with images

Paris art world with his paintings of peasant life. To artists and viewers accustomed to the classical traditions promoted by the French academies of art, Courbet's style was coarse and his subjects were common.

Courbet's belief that the artist must paint "real and existing things" influenced the next generation of French painters, which included Edouard Manet (1832–1883), sometimes called the father of modern art, and Edgar Degas (1834–1917). When Manet gave a painting the title *Olympia*, the image depicted, not the classical goddess of that name, but a prostitute. Degas, meanwhile, took for subjects the clients of Paris bars, ballet dancers rehearsing, and spontaneous scenes from the site of his favorite pastime, the racetrack.

Although France dominated European art, painting was also changing elsewhere. In England, a group of young artists formed a brotherhood to turn against what they saw as frivolous art and return to the

Mother and Her Child was painted by the American artist Mary Cassatt. Cassatt lived for a time in Paris, where she came under the influence of the Impressionists.

of the American Civil War that showed the influence of the documentary photographers who followed the conflict, such as Mathew Brady (1823–1896).

Impressionists

Some artists believed that photography made painting's concern with realism redundant. They set out to capture not a realistic depiction but their own vision, not what they *knew* they were looking at but what they actually *saw*. The French artists who led the movement, who came to be known as Impressionists, drew on the work of Degas and Manet, who themselves were sometimes considered part of the movement. The group's name dates from 1874, when they showed their work at the Salon des Refusés, a regular exhibition set up by artists whose work had been turned down by the official academic exhibitions.

Despite diverse styles and approaches, the Impressionists shared a desire to achieve naturalism and portray commonplace subjects. At the center of the group was Claude Monet (1840–1926), whose painting *Impression: Sunrise* gave the movement its name when it was used mockingly by a critic.

Monet applied pale colors onto specially prepared white canvas, which enhanced his disjointed brushwork. Toward the end of the century, Monet worked on series of paintings of a single subject: a cathedral, a haystack, a pond. He painted the same view at different times of day, swapping canvases as the light changed, to illustrate how his perception changed. He once said, "The principal subject in a painting is light." Other leading Impressionists include the Frenchmen Auguste Renoir and Camille Pissarro, the Englishman Alfred Sisley, and the American Mary Cassatt.

The Post-Impressionists

The term Post-Impressionism seems to imply that the movement it describes followed on from the Impressionists. In fact, the movements existed side by side. The leading Post-Impressionist, Paul Cézanne (1839–1906), was friends with Manet, Degas, and Pissarro, who was his biggest influence. More concerned with classical

This bronze bust of Richard Wagner stands outside the theater he built in Bayreuth, in Bavaria, specifically to stage his "total artworks."

This photograph of a haystack was taken by the photographic pioneer William Henry Fox Talbot and published in 1844. The camera's ability to reproduce effects such as the shadow cast by the ladder convinced many artists that realism was no longer a necessary aim in painting.

composition than the Impressionists, Cézanne also wanted to portray on canvas the structure of real things studied with great concentration. The appearance of his paintings, in which he places patches of color side by side to build up an object, looks forward to abstract painting and to the geometric shapes of the cubist movement of the early twentieth century.

Cross-Fertilization in the Arts

Cézanne had grown up with the influential novelist Émile Zola, and the two remained friends until Cézanne took offense at what he took to be a portrayal of himself in one of Zola's novels. Such a friendship was far from unique. Parisian culture was marked by friendships between painters, writers, sculptors, composers, and other creators. Ideas from one medium often influenced another. Impressionist painting, for example, had a parallel in music, where Claude Debussy (1862–1918) abandoned traditional melody in favor of shimmering effects and chords.

Other painters owed a debt to the symbolist poets—Stéphane Mallarmé (1842–

1898), Arthur Rimbaud (1854–1891), and Paul Verlaine (1844–1896)—who championed the imagination as the source of creativity. They used words for their symbolic rather than concrete meaning and believed that conveying emotion was more important than describing events. Painters such as Gustave Moreau (1826–1898) echoed the poets with emotive colors and stylized mythological and imagined scenes.

Van Gogh and Gauguin

The Dutch-born painter Vincent Van Gogh (1853–1890) and his friend Paul Gauguin (1848–1903) followed the principles of symbolism but painted from life. Van Gogh was beset by periods of madness, and he sold only one painting in his entire life, although today he is one of the most popular of all artists. The dark side of Van Gogh's vision is never far away in his work. His last painting, *Cornfields with Flight of Birds* (1890), shows a flock of crows filling a darkening sky. Soon after finishing it, Van Gogh killed himself.

Gauguin's paintings are a complete contrast. In a desire to escape France and his

family, Gauguin traveled to the Polynesian island of Tahiti. He developed a primitive style heavily influenced by sources such as ancient Egyptian and Cambodian sculpture. Gauguin's popularizing of such art eventually influenced virtually every major movement of twentieth-century art.

Literary Parallels

As painting adopted unfashionable subject matter, literature went through a similar change. Again, the lead came from France, where it was pioneered by Gustave Flaubert (1821–1880). Flaubert's greatest novel, *Madame Bovary* (1857), based on a short newspaper story, marked the beginning of a new type of literature. In telling his story of a provincial doctor's wife, her love affair, and its tragic conclusion, Flaubert aimed to be as objective as possible. He believed that an author should attempt to erase his or her personality from a story and present only objective details, without telling the reader how to interpret them.

Madame Bovary was first published not as a single book but in installments in a magazine. Such serial publishing was very common at the time. There was a huge readership for relatively cheap magazines, and a continuing serial could boost circulation, particularly when it used elements of melodrama to create cliffhanging endings.

The leading British novelist Charles Dickens (1812–1870) adapted his stories according to the circulation figures. When readers began to stop buying *Martin Chuzzlewit*, for example, Dickens suddenly sent the hero on a trip to the United States to rekindle their interest. Despite his commitment to commercial success, Dickens also waged an unremitting crusade against social ills. In *Hard Times* (1865), he created a bitter condemnation of the ills of industrial society. Such powerful social criticism became a staple of literature later in the century.

Zola and the Dreyfus Affair

As the century progressed, writers' desire to provide details to support the apparent realism and objectivity of their stories led to the creation of works of an epic scale. In Russia, Fyodor Dostoyevsky (1821–1881) and Lev Tolstoy (1828–1910) chronicled

Haystack at Sunset was painted in 1891 by the Impressionist Claude Monet. Rejecting photographic realism, Monet painted the patches of light and color he actually saw rather than the "real" shape of the haystack.

In *Sunflowers*, the artist Vincent Van Gogh used his characteristic vibrant colors and dramatic brushstrokes.

and sent to prison on Devil's Island. While newspapers and public opinion condemned Dreyfus as a symbol of the disloyalty of French Jews, evidence grew that the officer was innocent. In 1898, Zola wrote an open letter to a newspaper that took its title from its opening words, "J'accuse"—"I accuse." Zola accused the army of covering up Dreyfus's innocence and letting the real culprit go free. Zola was tried and found guilty of libel. Public opinion began to change, however, and calls for a retrial grew. It was granted in 1899 and, although Dreyfus was again found guilty, he was pardoned. In 1906, his name was cleared, and he was reinstated in the army.

The Dreyfus affair—called *l'affaire* in France—split France between right-wing nationalists and left-wingers opposed to the power of the army. The controversy it began left France weakened as World War I approached.

The Spread of Fashion

Paris remained at the heart of European culture. In the 1860s it became the world's fashion center after the English designer Charles Frederick Worth opened his shop in the city in 1858. Worth began haute couture, or high fashion, creating gowns for society women such as the French empress Eugénie. Fashion spread from Paris throughout the world thanks to an increase in the number and circulation of women's magazines, which carried illustrations of current fashions. After 1863, more practical magazines also included tissue-paper clothing patterns that allowed provincial or home dressmakers to make their own versions of the latest fashions. In America, *Harper's Bazar*—later *Harper's Bazaar*—began in 1867. In Britain, cheap weeklies such as *Home Notes* and *Home Companion* were influential in teaching women about matters such as child care and nutrition.

Architecture and Engineering

In 1889, a new structure rose above Paris as part of an exhibition that showcased French innovation. Intended for demolition after a year, the Eiffel Tower proved so popular that it still stands. At 1,050 feet, the tower was the world's tallest building until the Chrysler Building was completed in New York in 1931. Using the new building material of choice, steel, the tower became a symbol of an urban progress that it seemed would never stop.

Another expression of urban excitement came in the 1890s with the emergence of art nouveau. Originating in Belgium in 1892, the movement spread to cities such

urban and aristocratic life, respectively, in long novels. In France, Émile Zola followed his predecessor Honoré de Balzac (1799–1850), who attempted to present a picture of modern French society in a series of eighty-five novels called *La Comédie humaine,* "the human comedy." In the same way, Zola created a twenty-volume series of novels, *Les Rougon-Macquart,* the story of three branches of the same family.

The books illustrated Zola's belief that a person's behavior is determined by his or her environment and parentage. Because the individual has little opportunity to decide his or her own fate, Zola refuses to pass judgment on human actions. Zola's portrayal of industrial society and its indifference to the individual's struggle had a huge influence on the modern novel.

Zola is almost as famous for his political activities as for his novels, particularly in the Dreyfus affair that rocked France in the last decade of the century. Alfred Dreyfus was a French army officer who in 1894 was convicted of selling secrets to the Germans

as Paris, Berlin, Glasgow, and Vienna. The ornate style incorporated modern materials such as iron and glass for external decoration. It may still be seen in the wrought ironwork of many stations on the Paris and Vienna subways, which around 1900 were being extended into the city suburbs.

Vienna and European Music

If Paris stood for excitement, Austrian artists increasingly saw Vienna, capital of the Austro-Hungarian Empire, as backward looking and stagnant. In 1898 they formed the Secession movement, led by the painter Gustav Klimt, to encourage modern art.

Vienna was home to some of the most creative minds in Europe, including the

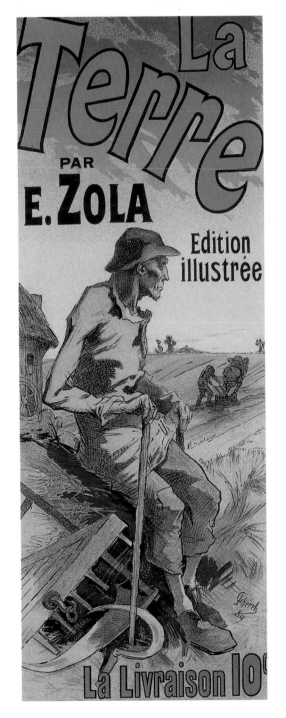

This photograph shows Alfred Dreyfus in his army uniform around 1890.

pioneering psychoanalyst Sigmund Freud (1856–1939) (*see 6:849*). In particular, Vienna lay at the heart of European music. From the 1860s to the 1890s, it was home to Johannes Brahms, whose passionate music continued the classical tradition of Beethoven (*see 5:644*). At the end of the century, the city was home to Gustav Mahler, whose epic orchestral works combined innovative techniques and a romantic sensibility. Mahler suffered virulent anti-Semitic attacks, and in 1908 he moved to New York. Soon a younger Viennese composer, Arnold Schoenberg, would begin experimenting with atonal music, which largely rejected classical traditions.

Elsewhere in Europe, the German Richard Wagner (1813–1883) attempted to create a new type of "total artwork," which

This French poster from the 1890s advertises an illustrated edition of *La Terre* (The Earth) by Émile Zola. Zola's novel painted a controversially harsh and sordid picture of the lives of French peasants.

847

This subway station entrance was built in the art nouveau style in Paris in the 1890s. It features the wrought-iron, glass, and stylized lettering that characterized the style.

combined poetry, dance, stagecraft, and music. In *The Ring of the Nibelung*, Wagner changed the course of music with a cycle of four operas that used myth as the basis of an epic of the German people. Wagner remains a highly controversial figure. In Italy, meanwhile, the opera composer Giuseppe Verdi spoke for the Italian people during their campaign for unification in the 1860s and in the new country's early years.

The Fin de Siècle

The last decades of the nineteenth century are described by a French term, the fin de siècle. Literally meaning "the end of the century," the term has a complex and contradictory meaning. It implies both the hedonistic gaiety of Europe's social elite and the sense of unease and foreboding that seemed to gather over the continent, as exposed in such divisive incidents as the Dreyfus affair.

On one hand, the fin de siècle was glittering, decadent, and extravagant. In London, Berlin, Vienna, and Paris, Europe's aristocratic elite escaped into an endless round of fashionable parties. The French author Marcel Proust (1871–1922), the author of the thirteen-volume *A la recherche du temps perdu*, captured the frivolity and inconsequentiality of such a life. In order to write it, Proust withdrew from society to his bedroom, where he devoted his life to his masterwork.

Other artists sought escape by deliberately disengaging their work from any social or political purpose. The Irish wit Oscar Wilde (1854–1900) adopted a doctrine of aestheticism—"art for art's sake"—which argued that the only purpose of art was to create beauty. Wilde entertained and scandalized his audiences in London and the United States. Asked if he had anything to declare at customs in New York, he reputedly replied, "Only my genius."

Sigmund Freud and the Inner Self

One of the most profound influences on the arts in the late nineteenth and early twentieth centuries came from medicine. In the 1880s and 1890s, the Austrian doctor Sigmund Freud (1856–1939) developed a new way of treating his emotionally disturbed patients, many of whom came from among Vienna's urban middle class. In 1896, Freud coined the word *psychoanalysis* to describe his new technique, which involved encouraging patients to express random thoughts while the analyst picks up pointers to guide the patients to reveal memories and thoughts they are not consciously aware of possessing. The technique and Freud's theories of human behavior revolutionized the way human beings understood themselves and each other.

Freud believed that what people think and how they behave is all conditioned by external influences, by things that have happened in the real world. Most of these experiences occur while people are very young. Freud believed that they were usually concerned with sex and sexual fears or desire. Freud believed that, in emotionally disturbed people such as hysterics or neurotics, these influential experiences were so painful that the conscious brain represses their memory. Instead, they are remembered in the unconscious. Freud believed that valuable clues to the workings of the unconscious came from such everyday events as stuttering over a word or name or making slips of the tongue, which today are known as Freudian slips.

Freud's interest in the unconscious also led him to study dreams. His 1899 work *The Interpretation of Dreams* argued that dreams are a kind of wish fulfillment that mingle fragments of recent, everyday experience with deep-seated wishes from childhood. Because those wishes are sometimes disturbing, dreams censor them, for instance by substituting one image as a symbol for another.

Freud proposed techniques to interpret the symbolism of apparently incomprehensible dreams. He wrote: "The interpretation of dreams is the royal road to a knowledge of the unconscious activities of the mind." Freud's belief acknowledged the importance artists such as the symbolists placed on images and dreams but also attempted to link them to real events in the everyday world. He believed that they could be explained by science.

Many of Freud's theories were criticized or dismissed by later psychologists. Even his assistant Carl Jung (1875–1961), himself an influential psychologist, disagreed with Freud's concentration on a child's relation with its parents. Jung instead proposed that, as well as a personal unconscious, members of a culture also share a collective unconscious. In contrast to Freud's emphasis on science, Jung was also interested in the paranormal and occult. Other critics of Freud's work explain adult behavior in terms of genetics or physiological factors or refuse to accept that adult behavior is wholly explicable in terms of one's childhood.

Nevertheless, Freud's work changed permanently the way humankind understood its dreams, desires, and fears. His theories of the unconscious and his emphasis on sex paved the way for artists and writers of the twentieth century to explore the inner life of the individual. Their influence on the arts and on everyday life remains strong today.

This photograph of Sigmund Freud was taken in England in 1939, the year of his death, after he had fled Austria to avoid persecution by the Nazis, who had annexed his homeland the previous year.

849

Edvard Munch (1863–1944) painted *Anxiety* in 1894. The painting was part of a series Munch called *The Frieze of Life* that intended to show "the poetry of life, love, and death."

This playbill shows Nijinsky, the principal dancer of the Ballet Russe. The dance company, which arrived in Paris in 1909, introduced western audiences to a new kind of ballet, expressed by Nijinsky's twisting, sinuous movements.

Alienation

Amid the exuberance of the fin de siècle, a sense of unease grew across Europe. Creators expressed the feeling of being an outsider. Such feelings had been prefigured by the German philosopher Friedrich Nietzsche (1844–1900). Nietzsche's argument that the "superman" was free to create his own moral code implied that some people existed outside society. Another popular philosophy, theosophy, reflected a revived interest in the occult.

The alienation of modern life received some of its starkest expressions in such works of the Norwegian artist Edvard Munch as *The Scream* (1893) and *Anxiety* (1894). The plays of Munch's compatriot Henrik Ibsen (1828–1906) set moral analysis in realistic, middle-class backgrounds. *A Doll's House* (1897) shocked audiences with its portrayal of the disintegration of a marriage. The German novelist Thomas Mann (1875–1955) echoed the theme in his 1901 *Buddenbrooks*, which traced the declining fortunes of a family.

Pointers to the Future

By the start of the twentieth century, creators seeking ways to express the modern world had broken away from the traditions that had long dominated creative activity. Pablo Picasso (1881–1973) and Georges Braque (1882–1963) created cubist paintings of disjointed, geometric shapes. In Russia, the artist Wassily Kandinsky (1866–1944), deciding that one of his paintings looked better lying on its side, took the first steps toward entirely abstract art that no longer tried to represent an external subject. In 1913, the Armory Show in New York City announced the arrival of modernism in the United States.

In music, Schoenberg's experiments with atonality were paralleled by the work of a young Russian composer, Igor Stravinsky (1882–1971). The premiere of Stravinsky's ballet *The Rite of Spring*, staged by the Ballet Russe in Paris in 1913, ended in riots as the audience expressed its displeasure at the rhythmic, repetitive score.

Paris was also the stage for what was perhaps the most informative pointer to the arts of the new century. In 1896, audience members fled in terror at the screening of an early movie, showing a railroad train apparently about to crash through the screen. The first-ever movie had been shown the previous year by the inventors of cinematography, the Lumière brothers. Like photography before it, the movies would change for ever the way creators portrayed the world (*see 7:951*).

Time Line

EUROPE	NORTH AND SOUTH AMERICA	ASIA AND AFRICA
1804 Uprising in Serbia against Ottoman rule	**1804** Haiti gains independence from Spain	**1805** Egyptians rebel against Ottoman rule and install Muhammad Ali as leader. Scottish explorer Mungo Park explores course of the Niger River.
1806 Russia invades Ottoman territory in Balkans	**1806** Venezuelan patriot Francisco de Miranda leads unsuccessful rebellion against Spanish rule	**1806** British capture Cape Colony from Dutch
1807 Britain bans slave trade. Napoleon invades Portugal: royal family flees to Brazil.		**1807** Ottoman sultan Selim III overthrown by Janissaries
1808 Napoleon invades Spain and makes his brother Joseph king	**1808** United States bans slave trade	
	1810 Spanish viceroy in Argentina overthrown. Catholic priest Miguel Hidalgo begins peasant uprising in Mexico. Bernardo O'Higgins leads attempted rebellion in Chile. Francisco de Miranda leads second rebellion in Venezuela and becomes dictator.	
	1811 Mexican peasant uprising defeated; Hidalgo executed.	
1812 Spanish assembly proclaims a liberal constitution	**1812** Spanish regain power in Venezuela. Simón Bolívar replaces Miranda as leader of independence movement.	
	1813 Bolívar's soldiers enter Caracas	
1814 The Netherlands bans the slave trade	**1814** Spanish troops recapture Caracas. Bolívar flees to Jamaica.	
	1815 Heir to Portuguese throne, Dom Jão, gives Brazil equal status with Portugal	
	1816 Dom Jão becomes king of Portugal and Brazil	
	1817 Bolívar returns to Venezuela. Argentinian patriot José de San Martín captures capital of Chile from Spanish.	
	1818 Bernardo O'Higgins becomes first independent ruler of Chile	**1818** Shaka Zulu becomes king of the Zulus
1819 "Peterloo massacre" in England: soldiers kill eleven at reform meeting	**1819** Bolívar captures Bogotá, capital of Colombia	
1820 Mutiny of Spanish army in Cádiz, weakening Spanish control of South America	**1820** San Martín attacks Peru from the sea	
1821 Greek revolt against Ottoman rule	**1821** Mexico gains independence from Spain. Bolívar becomes president of Gran Colombia and conquers rest of Venezuela. Portuguese prince Dom Pedro becomes regent of Brazil.	

1800 —
1810 —
1820 —

19th Century	20th Century

EUROPE	NORTH AND SOUTH AMERICA	ASIA AND AFRICA
	1822 Dom Pedro proclaimed emperor of Brazil. Bolívar's forces conquer Ecuador.	
	1823 Federation of Central American Republics formed. Mexico becomes a republic. O'Higgins resigns in Chile. U.S. president James Monroe proclaims Monroe Doctrine.	
1824 Royal Society for the Prevention of Cruelty to Animals founded in Britain	**1824** Bolívar's forces defeat Spanish in Peru	**1824** Saudis rebel against Ottoman rule and establish Arabian kingdom
1825 Labor unions legalized in Britain	**1825** Portugal acknowledges Brazil's independence	**1826** Ottoman sultan Mahmut II announces plans for European-style army
1827 Battle of Navarino: ships of Russia, France, and Britain destroy Ottoman navy		**1828** Mahmut II orders adoption of fez in place of turban
1829 Roman Catholics allowed to sit in British Parliament for first time since English Civil War	**1829** Mexican general Santa Anna defeats Spanish attempt to reconquer Mexico. Argentinian landowner Juan Manuel Rosas seizes governorship of Buenos Aires.	**1829** Russians force Ottomans to surrender territory in the Balkans and Anatolia
1830 Ottomans recognize autonomy of Serbia. July Revolution in France overthrows King Charles X.	**1830** Venezuela and Ecuador secede from United States of Gran Colombia; Bolívar resigns and dies. Indian Removal Act passed in the United States.	**1830** French force occupies Algiers
	1831 Brazilian emperor Pedro I abdicates. His five-year-old son succeeds as Pedro II.	**1831** French foreign legion founded. Egyptians under Muhammad Ali invade Syria.
1832 Reform Act passed in Britain	**1832** Rosas begins campaign against Indians in Argentina	**1832** Algerian tribes launch jihad against French invaders
	1833 New constitution adopted in Chile	
1834 French novelist Honoré de Balzac publishes *Le Père Goriot*	**1835** Rosas extends rule over most of Argentina. Uprising in Texas against Mexican rule.	**1835** Boer Great Trek begins. Japanese artist Katsushika Hokusai publishes *A Hundred Views of Mount Fuji*.
	1836 Siege of the Alamo: Santa Anna defeats Texan garrison. Battle of San Jacinto: Texans achieve independence.	
1839 Britain bans slavery. First photographic processes announced. English novelist Charles Dickens completes publication of *Oliver Twist*.	**1838** Santa Anna expels French from Veracruz	**1839** Ottoman Edict of Gulhane proclaims equality of all subjects. Boers proclaim republic of Natal. First Opium War begins between Britain and China.
		1841 Ottomans proclaim Muhammad Ali's family hereditary rulers of Egypt
1842 First performance of opera *Nabucco*, the first major success for Italian composer Giuseppe Verdi		**1842** Treaty of Nanking ends First Opium War
1843 First Christmas card printed in Britain		**1843** Britain annexes Natal

	19th Century		20th Century

EUROPE	NORTH AND SOUTH AMERICA	ASIA AND AFRICA
1844 French artist Gustave Courbet begins exhibiting realistic paintings of peasant life	**1845** Texas becomes part of United States **1846** United States declares war on Mexico **1847** United States defeats Santa Anna and occupies Mexico City	**1844** United States gains trade access to China **1846** Britain allowed to establish Christian mission in Okinawa
1848 First public health act in Britain. Karl Marx and Friedrich Engels publish *The Communist Manifesto*.	**1848** Mexico cedes all land north of the Rio Grande to the United States. California Gold Rush begins.	
1850 English artist Dante Gabriel Rossetti forms the Pre-Raphaelite Brotherhood		**1850** Hung Hsiu-ch'uan begins Taiping Rebellion in China
1851 First performance of Verdi's opera *Rigoletto*	**1852** Rosas overthrown in Argentina	**1852** Boers proclaim republic of Transvaal
1853 Start of Crimean War. German composer Richard Wagner begins work on opera cycle, *The Ring of the Nibelung*.	**1853** Gadsden Purchase transfers further land from Mexico to United States	**1853** Taiping capital established in Nanking. U.S. flotilla arrives in Japan seeking a trade treaty.
		1854 Japan signs treaty opening two ports to U.S. trade. Boers proclaim republic of Orange Free State.
1855 English novelist Anthony Trollope publishes *The Warden*		**1855** English explorer David Livingstone reaches and names Victoria Falls
1856 German-English scientist William Siemens invents new type of gas-fired furnace, leading to the open-hearth process for steel-making		**1856** Start of Second Opium War between Britain and China
1857 French novelist Gustave Flaubert publishes *Madame Bovary*. French poet Charles Baudelaire publishes *Les Fleurs du Mal*.	**1857** Mexican constitution reduces power of army and church	
1858 Great Stink in London		
1860 Bessemer process for making iron into steel patented	**1860** Liberals win Mexican civil war. Pony Express inaugurated in United States.	**1860** British and French defeat Taiping rebels at Shanghai. End of Second Opium War.
1861 Serfs gain freedom in Russia	**1861** Electric telegraph replaces Pony Express. Benito Juárez elected first civilian president of Mexico. Civil war begins in United States.	
	1862 Homestead Act passed in United States. Napoleon III invades Mexico.	
1863 English novelist Charles Kingsley publishes *The Waterbabies*		**1863** Japanese shogun abolishes restrictions on daimyo
1864 First International formed: international trade union conference. French artist Édouard Manet paints *Olympia*.	**1864** Habsburg archduke Maximilian of Austria becomes emperor of Mexico	

19th Century	20th Century

	EUROPE	NORTH AND SOUTH AMERICA	ASIA AND AFRICA
1865	**1865** World's first department store opens in Paris. Dickens publishes *Hard Times*.	**1865** Civil war ends in United States. U.S. president Abraham Lincoln assassinated. Thirteenth Amendment to the U.S. Consitution bans slavery and leads to establishment of Freedmen's Bureau. Ku Klux Klan founded.	**1865** Kiangnan arsenal opened in Shanghai
	1866 Russian novelist Fyodor Dostoevsky publishes *Crime and Punishment*	**1866** Napoleon III withdraws French troops from Mexico. In the United States, rioters in Memphis and New Orleans kill African Americans.	**1866** First western-style shipyard opened in China. In Japan, four daimyo families ally against the shogunate.
	1867 Paris Exhibition. French novelist Émile Zola publishes *Thérèse Raquin*.	**1867** Execution of Maximilian in Mexico; Juárez re-elected president. Reconstruction Act in United States.	
	1868 English novelist Wilkie Collins publishes *The Moonstone*	**1868** U.S. president Andrew Johnson impeached by Congress. Fourteenth Amendment gives equality before law to all U.S. citizens. First African American elected to U.S. Congress.	**1868** Meiji Restoration in Japan ends shogun era
	1869 Russian novelist Leo Tolstoy completes publication of *War and Peace*	**1869** Ku Klux Klan goes underground. First U.S. transcontinental railroad completed. American author Louisa M. Alcott publishes *Little Women*.	**1869** Suez Canal opens
1870	**1870** Start of Franco-Prussian War	**1870** Fifteenth Amendment gives former slaves the right to vote	
	1871 Paris Commune: workers' government in Paris. Treaty of Frankfurt ends Franco-Prussian War: France loses Alsace and part of Lorraine. Germany unified.	**1871** U.S. government tries to suppress Ku Klux Klan. World's first steam-powered, elevated railway built in New York. U.S. artist Thomas Eakins paints *Max Schmitt in a Single Scull*.	**1871** Japanese nobles surrender land to emperor, ending feudal system. Japanese mission to study Western government and industry. Welsh journalist H. M. Stanley meets Livingstone in Africa.
	1872 Russian anarchist Mikhail Bakunin expelled from First International	**1872** Death of Benito Juárez, president of Mexico	
	1873 French poet Arthur Rimbaud publishes *A Season in Hell*		
	1874 French artist Claude Monet paints *Impression: Sunrise*, the first Impressionist painting. First collection of Impressionist work shown at Salon des Refusés in Paris. Wagner completes *The Ring of the Nibelung*.	**1874** Introduction of barbed wire fencing onto Great Plains in United States	
			1875 Railroad completed between Tokyo and Yokohama
	1876 First International dissolved. Tolstoy completes *Anna Karenina*. German composer Johannes Brahms completes his first symphony. French artist Edgar Degas paints *The Dancing Class*.	**1876** Battle of the Little Big Horn: Sioux and Cheyenne warriors wipe out a U.S. cavalry detachment. Election of Rutherford B. Hayes as U.S. president marks end of Reconstruction. Central Park opened in New York City. Porfirio Díaz becomes president of Mexico.	**1876** Britain and France establish joint protectorate over Egypt. New Ottoman constitution. King Leopold of Belgium founds International Association of the Congo. First train service in China.
	1877 Russia renews war against Ottoman Empire. Author Anna Sewell publishes *Black Beauty*.	**1877** American inventor Thomas Edison patents the phonograph	**1877** Samurai rising in Japan
	1878 Treaty of Berlin tries to bring stability to Balkans		**1878** Modern coal mine opened in China. Last Taiping rebellion crushed.
		1879 Edison develops first practical light bulb	**1879** Zulus defeat British at Ishandhlwana

19th Century	20th Century

EUROPE	NORTH AND SOUTH AMERICA	ASIA AND AFRICA
1880 Dostoevsky completes publication of *The Brothers Karamazov*	**1880** American author Joel Chandler Harris publishes *Uncle Remus*	**1880** Start of First Boer War
		1881 End of First Boer War: British accept independence of Transvaal. French establish protectorate over Tunisia.
1882 French artist Auguste Renoir exhibits *Au Moulin de la Galette*	**1883** Brooklyn Bridge completed. End of War of the Pacific: Chile gains nitrate fields from Peru.	**1882** British take control of Egypt
1885 Berlin Conference of European powers divides overseas spheres of influence. Zola publishes *Germinal*. German philosopher Friedrich Nietzsche completes publication of *Thus Spake Zarathustra*.		**1885** French protectorate over Annam recognized by China. Mahdi drives British out of Sudan.
1887 Zola publishes *La Terre*		**1886** South African Gold Rush
1888 Dutch-born artist Vincent van Gogh paints *Sunflowers*; also (c. 1888) French artist Paul Cézanne paints *Still Life with Commode*, anticipating cubist principles	**1888** Brazil bans slavery, the last South American country to do so. Apache chief Geronimo captured. Kodak make first box camera.	
1889 Second International formed. Eiffel Tower constructed in Paris, France. Czech-Austrian composer Gustav Mahler completes his first symphony.	**1889** Brazilian emperor Pedro II deposed; Brazil becomes a republic	**1889** Parliamentary constitution adopted in Japan
1890 Van Gogh paints his last picture, *Cornfields with Flight of Birds*	**1890** Sherman Antitrust Act passed in United States. Ghost Dance movement among Native Americans. Sioux massacred at Wounded Knee.	
1891 English novelist Arthur Conan Doyle publishes *The Adventures of Sherlock Holmes*		**1891** French artist Paul Gauguin goes to Tahiti to paint
1892 Cholera epidemic in Hamburg. Art nouveau movement begins in Belgium.	**1892** Populist, or People's, Party formed in United States	
1893 Independent Labour Party formed in Britain. Norwegian artist Edvard Munch paints *The Scream*.	**1893** Financial crash in United States	
1894 French composer Claude Debussy writes *Prélude á l'après-midi d'un faune*	**1894** Pullman Strike by railroad workers in United States	**1894** Turks begin repression of Armenians. Japan sends troops to Korea. Outbreak of Sino-Japanese War.
1895 First production of the stage comedy *The Importance of Being Earnest* by Irish writer Oscar Wilde. World's first movie theater opens in Paris.	**1895** Revolt in Cuba against Spanish rule. World's first electric-powered, elevated railway built in Chicago.	**1895** Treaty of Shimonoseki ends Sino-Japanese War. Jameson Raid in southern Africa.
1896 *Daily Mail*, a mass-circulation newspaper, founded in Britain		**1896** Battle of Adowa: Ethiopians defeat Italian army
1897 First performance of the play *A Doll's House* by Norwegian dramatist Henrik Ibsen. French artist Camille Pissarro paints *Boulevard Montmartre*.		
1898 Zola publishes article "J'accuse" on the Dreyfus affair. Viennese artists form the Secession movement.	**1898** Spanish-American War	**1898** "Hundred Days of Reform" in China defeated by conservative empress

19th Century	20th Century

EUROPE	NORTH AND SOUTH AMERICA	ASIA AND AFRICA

ASIA AND AFRICA

Battle of Omdurman: British defeat Mahdi in Sudan. Fashoda incident between British and French forces in Africa.

1899 Boxer Rebellion begins in China. Boers invade Natal: outbreak of Second Boer War.

1900 International force sacks Beijing

1901 End of Boxer Rebellion in China

1902 Japanese alliance with Britain. End of Second Boer War.

1904 Russo-Japanese War begins

1905 Japanese defeat Russians at Mukden and Tsushima

1907 Deaths of dowager empress of China and emperor Tzu-hsi. In Southwest Africa, the Herero people rebel against German rule.

1908 Young Turk revolt; Ottoman sultan Abdülhamid forced to restore constitution

1909 Sultan Abdülhamid deposed

1910 Japan annexes Korea

1912 Last Manchu emperor of China abdicates; China becomes a republic. South African Native National Congress formed.

EUROPE

1899 Last European cholera epidemic. Austrian doctor Sigmund Freud publishes *The Interpretation of Dreams*.

1900

1901 German novelist Thomas Mann publishes *Buddenbrooks*

1905 Debussy completes orchestral piece *La Mer*

1907 Hague Peace Conference. Spanish artist Pablo Picasso paints *Les Demoiselles d'Avignon*, the first important cubist painting.

1908 Austrian composer Arnold Schoenberg starts experimenting with atonal music. French novelist Marcel Proust begins to write *À la recherche du temps perdu*.

1909 Ballet Russe arrives in Paris

1910 Russian artist Wassily Kandinsky starts experimenting with abstract painting

1910

1912 French artist Georges Braques completes painting *Man with a Guitar*

1913 First performance of ballet *The Rite of Spring*, with music by Russian composer Igor Stravinsky

1914 Start of World War I

1917 Russian Revolution

1918 End of World War I in Europe

NORTH AND SOUTH AMERICA

1901 U.S. president William McKinley assassinated

1902 Coal strike in Pennsylvania

1903 Panama gains independence from Colombia

1910 Mexican Revolution begins

1911 Porfirio Díaz forced to quit presidency of Mexico; Francisco Madero elected

1912 Theodore Roosevelt forms Progressive Party

1913 Victoriano Huerta overthrows Madero and becomes president of Mexico. Armory Show of modernist painting in New York.

1914 U.S. troops occupy Veracruz; Venustiano Carranza declares himself president of Mexico. Panama Canal opens.

1916 Pancho Villa kills U.S. citizens in New Mexico

1917 United States enters World War I. New constitution in Mexico.

1918 End of World War I in Europe

1917 South African Native National Congress becomes African National Congress

1919 End of World War I in Asia

19th Century	20th Century

Glossary

anarchism a political philosophy that argues against all forms of government in favor of free cooperation between members of society. Modern anarchist theories developed in the nineteenth century, when some of their supporters argued that violence was necessary to overthrow the existing order and establish anarchist society.

aristocracy the hereditary nobility of a state whose titles, status, and privilege may or may not bring them special political power.

art nouveau an ornate style of art and architecture that originated in Belgium in 1892 and featured long, flowing lines and stylized patterns of flowers and leaves. Art nouveau influenced the design of furniture, vases, glassware, jewelry, interior decoration, and poster and book illustration.

autocracy a system of government by a single ruler with no restraints on his or her behavior.

black codes various laws passed in former Confederate states after the U.S. Civil War to restrict the rights of African Americans, who might be banned from owning land, put in jail if unemployed, or punished for infringements by whipping. Congress countered the black codes by passing the Fourteenth Amendment, guaranteeing equality before the law, and the Reconstruction Act, which placed the South under military control.

bourgeoisie in Karl Marx's analysis of capitalist society, the class that owns and manages the means of production and distribution, such as factories and other businesses. The word is sometimes used as an equivalent for "middle class," particularly with reference to nineteenth-century society. *See also* class.

capitalism an economic system whose roots lay in the Early Modern period but which developed fully during the Industrial Revolution. In a capitalist economy, private individuals and companies control the production and distribution of goods and services, making profit in return for the investment of money, or capital.

carpetbaggers a Southern name for Northerners who moved in the Southern states in the Reconstruction era after the U.S. Civil War. The name referred to the bags in which they supposedly carried their belongings. *See also* Scalawags.

caudillo a Spanish word used to refer to Latin American dictators who gained political power through personal charisma, often after military command during wartime.

class a division of society whose members have in common similar degrees of wealth and status, and often share similar occupations. In industrial society, the most universal divisions are the upper class, the middle class, and the lower or working class. Class divisions were traditionally based on birth and heredity, but today more commonly reflect education, wealth, and occupation.

communism a political doctrine, based on the writings of Karl Marx (1818–1883) and Friedrich Engels (1820–1895), that shares with socialism the aim of creating a classless society. In Marxist theory, communism can be achieved only by the violent overthrow of capitalism and the establishment of working-class or proletarian rule. After the 1917 Russian Revolution, communism became the official ideology of the Soviet Union and directly or indirectly dominated much of the globe.

creoles people of Spanish descent born in Spain's American colonies. They are sometimes also called criollos.

daimyo Japanese feudal lords.

democracy a system of government based on the wishes of a majority of a nation's people. Citizens elect representatives such as members of Congress or members of Parliament to represent them in the decision-making process.

evolution the process by which living things have changed over time to create more highly adapted descendants. The theory of evolution was formulated in the mid–nineteenth century by the English naturalist Charles Darwin (1809–1882), who argued that evolution was the result of "natural selection," a process in which random mutations favor the survival of certain members of a species or of certain species over others.

free trade *See* laissez-faire.

Freedmen's Bureau a welfare agency set up to help ex-slaves in the aftermath of the U.S. Civil War. The bureau provided food, shelter, and educational opportunities, protected civil rights, and supervised work contracts.

gauchos South American cowboys, traditionally found on the plains or pampas of Argentina and Uruguay.

Ghost Dance a mystical Native American religious movement of the late nineteenth century that promised a restoration of traditional ways of life and the end of Euro-American domination. The movement became associated with Sioux resistance to U.S. control, which was crushed in 1890 at the Battle of Wounded Knee.

hacienda a Spanish word for a ranch, plantation, or farm with a dwelling house.

imperialism the policy or practice of nations obtaining and exploiting dependent territories, such as the nineteenth-century accumulation of African and Asian empires by many European powers. In "economic imperialism," powerful countries exploit weaker ones economically without claiming formal jurisdiction over them.

impressionism an influential artistic style that originated in painting in France in the 1860s. Impressionist painters tried to convey a faithful impression of a scene as perceived by the artist's eye rather than an image shaped by pre-formed assumptions or artistic tradition.

industrialization the development and concentration of industry as a major source of a region's wealth. After the Industrial Revolution of the nineteenth century, industry replaced agriculture and traditional crafts as the main economic activity in many parts of Europe and North America.

Islam a major world religion, founded in the sixth and seventh centuries by the prophet Muhammad (c. 570–632). The followers of Islam, called Muslims, worship one god, Allah. Islam is split into two branches. Shia Islam is popular in Iran. Sunni Islam dominates the rest of the Islamic world.

Janissaries an elite military corps in the Ottoman Empire, recruit mainly from young Christians taken as tribute from their parents. Established in the 1300s, they were noted for their discipline but later became a threat to the sultan's authority and were outlawed in 1826.

Ku Klux Klan a secret society, founded in 1865 by former Confederate soldiers, that aimed to preserve white supremacy by violence. Forced underground in the 1870s, the Klan re-emerged in the early twentieth century. Its current membership is probably about 6,000.

laissez-faire an influential economic theory developed by Adam Smith (1723–1790). Smith opposed tariffs and other governmental restraints on trade and argued that markets should be regulated only by the forces of supply and demand, which would encourage efficiency and economic progress. Laissez-faire shaped orthodox economic thinking in the eighteenth and nineteenth centuries.

liberalism a political philosophy valuing individual and economic freedom and equality that emerged in the eighteenth century in reaction to traditional privilege and oppressive government. Liberal thought was influential in establishing constitutional governments in Europe and America.

manifest destiny the nineteenth-century belief that the United States had both a right and a duty to govern all of North America. Manifest destiny was an important spur for U.S. expansion across the continent to the Pacific coast.

mestizo/mestiza a Latin American man or woman of mixed European and Native American parentage.

Mfecane a Zulu word for "crushing" that refers to a period of violence and upheaval among the peoples of southern Africa between 1819 and 1838, caused by the expansion of the Zulu and their displacement of other peoples over a large area.

modernism an artistic and literary movement that flourished in the Western world from about 1910 to about 1950. In prose, poetry, painting, and music, modernism rejected traditional techniques and rules in favor of abstraction and disjunction.

Monroe Doctrine the principle, asserted in 1823 by U.S. president James Monroe, that the United States would oppose new European colonial ventures in the Americas and would not tolerate European interference in the affairs of independent American countries. The doctrine effectively proclaimed U.S. primacy in the Americas and is still used as a justification for U.S. activity elsewhere in the hemisphere.

nationalism a political belief in the right of a people bound by language, history, and culture to rule itself in its own nation or state. Nationalism became a major force in European and South American politics in the nineteenth century and in Asia and Africa in the twentieth.

neoclassicism a style of art popular in late-eighteenth-century Europe that adopted the subject matter and style of ancient Greece and Rome by imitating classical sculptures and other artefacts and stressing the perceived values of classical cultures.

Orthodox Christianity the main form of Christianity in Greece, Russia, and many other parts of eastern Europe and western Asia. The Orthodox Church separated from Roman Catholicism because of longstanding differences in doctrine, especially concerning the authority of the pope.

Ottoman Empire a Muslim empire centered in Turkey, lasting from about 1300 to 1922. It was founded by the Ottoman Turks, a nomadic people from central Asia.

pampas the plains of southern South America, especially in Argentina.

peninsulares Spaniards living in Spanish America but born in Spain.

peon a Native American agricultural laborer in the Spanish empire in America. Peons had no land of their own and were tied by debt to working for their master.

plantation a large agricultural estate, usually in the Americas or Asia, on which European planters used native or slave labor to grow crops such as sugar cane or tobacco. The word plantation was also sometimes used to mean a new settlement in a colony, as in Plymouth Plantation.

proletariat in Karl Marx's theory of communism, the lowest class of capitalist society, the industrial workers who have nothing to sell but their labor. Marx believed that the proletariat, driven by intolerable living conditions, would lead the revolution to overthrow capitalism.

protectionism an economic policy in which governments impose restrictions such as high duties on imported goods in order to protect their own industries or agriculture from foreign competition. Protectionism is fundamentally opposed to doctrines of laissez-faire and free trade.

psychoanalysis an influential method of understanding the mind developed by the Austrian doctor Sigmund Freud (1856–1939). Freud emphasized the importance of the unconscious mind, which represses the early experiences that shape adult behavior.

republicanism the principle of having an elected or nominated head of state rather than a hereditary ruler.

scalawags a derogatory Southern term for local whites who cooperated with Northerners and African Americans in the Reconstruction era after the U.S. Civil War to bring social reform and pass civil rights legislation. *See also* carpetbaggers.

sharecropping a system of agricultural landholding in which tenant farmers give their landlords a share of the crops they grow rather than paying rent.

shogun in feudal times Japan's supreme military commander. By the fourteenth century, the shogun had become the country's real ruler rather than the emperor. The position was hereditary and passed through the Minamoto and Ashikaga families to the Tokugawa, who ruled from 1603 to 1867.

Social Darwinism an analysis of society and politics based on Charles Darwin's theory of evolution, which argues that natural selection creates superior and inferior individuals, races, or nations. The theory was used to justify policies such as Europe's colonization of Africa in the late nineteenth century.

socialism a political doctrine that aims to create a classless society by removing factories and businesses from private ownership for the good of all. Some socialists advocate state ownership, some local ownership, and some ownership by associations of workers. Although most socialists believe that the transition to socialism can be achieved through democratic processes, others argue that capitalism can only be ended by violent revolution.

symbolism a late-nineteenth-century literary movement promoted by French poets as a reaction against realism. Symbolism tried to convey emotions and ideas indirectly by the use of unexplained images.

temperance movement a social movement popular in the late nineteenth century that advocated complete abstinence from alcohol. Temperance organizations encouraged adherents to take pledges to abstain from alcohol.

totalitarianism a system of government in which the state controls every aspect of life and suppresses all political opposition.

trusts alliances formed between businesses to force prices up and bring costs down. Several U.S. industries, such as oil and steel, formed such anticompetitive associations to avoid laws against trade monopolies. Trusts were outlawed by the Sherman Antitrust Act of 1890.

utopianism a belief that an ideal human society can be achieved in which everyone is happy, all needs are met, and all talents are given full play. The word comes from the title of Thomas More's 1516 book *Utopia*, which imagined such a place.

viceroyalty a colony or region ruled by a viceroy on behalf of a king or queen.

working class the lowest class in industrial society. Members of this class work for wages and do some of the least prestigious jobs, such as manual work in industry or agriculture, operating checkouts in stores, or working in fast-food restaurants. *See also* proletariat.

Further Resources

The Shrinking Ottoman World

Brown, L. Carl. *Imperial Legacy: The Ottoman Imprint on the Balkans and the Middle East*. New York: Columbia University Press, 1997.

Godwin, J. *Lords of the Horizons: A History of the Ottoman Empire*. New York: Henry Holt & Co., 1999.

Gondicas, D., and Issawi, C., eds. *Ottoman Greeks in the Age of Nationalism: Politics, Economy, and Society in the Nineteenth Century*. Pennington, NJ: Darwin Press, 1998.

Kasaba, R. *The Ottoman Empire and the World Economy: The Nineteenth Century*. State University of New York Press, 1989.

Kent, M., ed. *The Great Powers and the End of the Ottoman Empire*. Ilford: Frank Cass & Co, 1995.

Palmer, A. W. *The Decline and Fall of the Ottoman Empire*. M. E. Evans and Co, 1994.

Revolution in Mexico

Eisenhower, J. S. D. *Intervention! The United States and the Mexican Revolution, 1913–1917*. London: W. W. Norton & Co., 1995.

Katz, F. *The Life and Times of Pancho Villa*. Stanford, CA: Stanford University Press, 1998.

Knight, A. *The Mexican Revolution: Porfirians, Liberals, and Peasants*. Lincoln, NE: University of Nebraska Press, 1990.

Tinkle, L. *13 Days to Glory: The Seige of the Alamo*. Texas A&M University Press, 1996.

Tutino, J. *From Insurrection to Revolution in Mexico: Social Bases of Agrarian Violence, 1750–1940*. Princeton, NJ: Princeton University Press, 1989.

Revolution in South America

Bethell, L., ed. *The Cambridge History of Latin America: Colonial Latin America, Vol. 2*. New York: Cambridge University Press, 1985.

Costeloe, M. P. *Response to Revolution: Imperial Spain and the Spanish American Revolutions, 1810–1840*. New York: Cambridge University Press, 1986.

Hooker, T. *The Armies of Bolívar and San Martín*. New York: Osprey Publishing Co., 1991.

Lynch, J. *The Spanish American Revolution, 1808–26*. London: W. W. Norton & Co., 1986.

Lynch, J., ed. *Latin American Revolutions, 1808–26: Old and New World Origins*. Norman, OK: University of Oklahoma Press, 1996.

South America After Independence

Bethell, L. *The Cambridge History of Latin America: From Independence to 1870*. New York: Cambridge University Press, 1985.

Bushnell, D. *The Emergence of Latin America in the Nineteenth Century*. New York: Oxford University Press, 1995.

Graham, R. *Independence in Latin America: A Comparative Approach*. New York: McGraw Hill Text, 1994.

Kingsbruner, J. *Independence in Spanish America: Civil Wars, Revolutions, and Underdevelopment*. Albuquerque, NM: University of New Mexico Press, 1994.

Rodriguez, J. E. *The Independence of Spanish America*. New York: Cambridge University Press, 1998.

China in the Nineteenth Century

Fay, P. W. *The Opium War, 1840–42: Barbarians in the Celestial Empire in the Early Part of the Nineteenth Century*. Chapel Hill, NC: University of North Carolina Press, 1998.

Paludan, A. *Chronicle of the Chinese Emperors: The Reign-by-Reign Record of the Rulers of Imperial China*. New York: Thames and Hudson, 1998.

Prazniak, R. *Of Camel Kings and Other Things: Rural Rebels Against Modernity in Late Imperial China*. Lanham, MD: Rowman and Littlefield, 1999

Schrecker, C. *Reform in Nineteenth Century China*. Cambridge, MA: Harvard University Press, 1976.

Spence, J. D. *God's Chinese Son: The Taiping Heavenly Kingdom of Hong Xinquan*. London: W. W. Norton & Co., 1996.

Nineteenth-Century Japan

Iriye, A. *Japan and the Wider World: From the Mid–Nineteenth Century to the Present*. Reading, MA: Addison Wesley Publishing Co., 1997.

Jansen, M. B., ed. *The Cambridge History of Japan: The Nineteenth Century*. New York: Cambridge University Press, 1989.

Kelly, W. W. *Deference and Defiance in Nineteenth-Century Japan*. Princeton, NJ: Princeton University Press, 1985.

Kornicki, P. F. *The Book in Japan: A Cultural History from the Beginnings to the Nineteenth Century*. Boston, MA: Brill Academic Publishers, 1997.

Mehl, M. *History and the State in Nineteenth-Century Japan*. New York: St. Martin's Press, 1998.

The Second Wave of Industrialization

Bradley, J. *Guns for the Tsar: American Technology and the Small Arms Industry in Nineteenth-Century Russia*. De Kalb, IL: Northern Illinois University Press, 1990.

Briggs, A. *Victorian Things*. Chicago: University of Chicago Press, 1989.

McCullogh, D. *The Great Bridge: The Epic Story of the Building of the Brooklyn Bridge*. New York: Simon and Schuster, 1983.

Morus, I. R. *Frankenstein's Children: Electricity, Exhibition, and Experiment in Early Nineteenth-Century London.* Princeton, NJ: Princeton University Press, 1998.

Late-Nineteenth-Century Society in the West
Barth, G. *City People: The Rise of Modern City Culture in Nineteenth-Century America.* New York: Oxford University Press, 1982.
Dale, P. A. *In Pursuit of a Scientific Culture: Science, Art, and Society in the Victorian Age.* Madison, WI: University of Wisconsin Press, 1990.
Kocka, J. *Bourgeois Society in Nineteenth-Century Europe.* Indianapolis, IN: Berg Publishing Ltd., 1994.
Marcus, S. *Apartment Stories: City and Home in Nineteenth-Century Paris and London.* Berkeley, CA: University of California Press, 1999.
Sante, L. *Low Life: Lures and Snares of Old New York.* New York: Vintage Books, 1992.
Schlereth, T. *Victorian America: Transformations in Everyday Life, 1876–1915.* New York: HarperCollins, 1991.

The Rise of Socialism
Brandt, W. *German Essays on Socialism in the Nineteenth Century.* New York: Continuum Publishing Groups, 1990.
Charlton, J. *The Chartists: The First National Workers Movement.* Oxford, UK: Pluto Press, 1997.
Docherty, J. C. *Historical Dictionary of Socialism.* Lanham, MD: Scarecrow Press, 1997.
Feurbach, L. *German Socialist Philosophy.* New York: Continuum Publishing Group, 1996.
Messer-Kruse, T. *The Yankee International: Marxism and the American Reform Tradition, 1848–1876.* Chapel Hill, NC: University of North Carolina Press, 1998.
Proudhon, P-J. *The General Idea of the Revolution in the Nineteenth Century.* Oxford, UK: Pluto Press, 1989.

The Scramble for Africa
Chamberlain, M. E. *The Scramble for Africa.* Reading, MA: Addison Wesley Publishing Co., 1974.
Curtin, P. D. *Disease and Empire: The Health of European Troops in the Conquest of Africa.* New York: Cambridge University Press, 1998.
Nutting, A. *Scramble for Africa: The Great Trek to the Boer War.* London: Constable and Co., 1994.
Oliver, O., and Atmore, A. *Africa Since 1800.* New York: Cambridge University Press, 1994.
Pakenham, T. *The Scramble for Africa: White Man's Conquest of the Dark Continent from 1876 to 1912.* New York: Random House, 1991.
Sagay, J. O. *Africa: A Modern History 1800–1975.* New York: Holmes and Maier Publishing, 1981.

The Triumph of the Dollar
Allison, R. J., ed. *America Eras: Development of the Industrial United States.* Detroit, MI: Gale Research, 1997.
Ambrose, S. E. *Crazy Horse and Custer: The Parallel Lives of Two American Warriors.* Anchor, 1996.
Foner, E. *America's Reconstruction: People and Politics After the Civil War.* Baton Rouge, LA: Louisiana State University Press, 1997.
Franklin, J. H. *Reconstruction After the Civil War.* Chicago, IL: University of Chicago Press, 1995.
Litwak, L. F. *Trouble in Mind: Black Southerners in the Age of Jim Crow.* New York: Knopf, 1998.
McCullogh, D. *Path Between the Seas: The Creation of the Panama Canal, 1870–1914.* New York: Simon and Schuster, 1978.
Morris, E. *The Rise of Theodore Roosevelt.* New York: Ballantine Books, 1988.
Traxel, D. *1898: The Birth of the American Century.* New York: Knopf, 1998
Ward, G. C., et al. *The West: An Illustrated History.* New York: Little Brown and Co., 1996

The Arts in the Late Nineteenth Century
Barnhill, G. B. *The Cultivation of Artists in Nineteenth-Century America.* New Castle, DE: Oak Knoll Press, 1997.
Bowe, N. G. *Art and the National Dream: The Search for Vernacular Expression in Turn of the Century Design.* Dublin: Irish Academic Press, 1993.
Canady, J. E. *Mainstreams of Modern Art.* Austin, TX: Holt, Rinehart & Winston, 1981.
Garb, T. *Sisters of the Brush: Women's Artistic Culture in Late-Nineteenth-Century Paris.* New Haven, CT: Yale University Press, 1994.
Herbert, R. L. *Impressionism: Art, Leisure, and Parisian Society.* New Haven, CT: Yale University Press, 1988.
Schwartz, V. R. *Spectacular Realities: Early Mass Culture in Fin-de-Siecle Paris.* Berkeley, CA: University of California Press, 1998.
Sternau, S. A. *Art Nouveau: The Spirit of the Belle Epoque.* Todtri Productions Ltd., 1998.
Thomson, B. *The Post-Impressionists.* London: Phaidon Press, 1995

Illustration Credits

(a = above, b = below, l = left, r = right)
AKG London: 724-725, 824a
Corbis: 775a, 775b, 786a, 791, 795a, 795b, 796, 810a, 814b, 815b, 840; Adam Woolfitt 843b; Alexander Burkatowski 842a; Asian Art & Archaeology, Inc 784, 785a; Austrian Archives 811; Bettmann 735a, 735b, 744b, 777, 787, 789, 815a, 830a, 833b, 834, 845; Christel Gerstenberg 739b; Dave G. Houser 835; Enzo & Paolo Ragazzini 753b; Gianni Dagli Orti 850b; H. Evans/Cordaiy Photo Library 813a; Historical Picture Archive 797, 820, 847b; Hulton Getty 767, 804; Illustrated London News 764, 773a, 785b; Jonathan Blair 733; Leonard de Selva 734, 803a; Michael Maslan Historic Photographs 727, 732, 779a, 779b, 782; Michael Nicholson 749; Michael T. Sedam 837b; Minnesota Historical Society 806, 837a; Museum of the City of New York 814a; National Gallery, London 790; Nik Wheeler 821b; Owen Franken 761; Pablo Corral V 755; Patrick Ward 821a; Paul Almasy 783, 788b, 848; Philadelphia Museum of Art 801a; Philip de Bay 730; Royal Ontario Museum 772, 780; Scientific American 773b; Stephanie Colasanti 803b; The National Archives 745, 786b; Wolfgang Kaehler 771
David King Collection: 812, 813b
E. T. Archive: 807
Hulton Getty: 729, 731b, 736, 788a, 792a, 792b, 793, 794, 798, 841, 844, 847a
The Image Bank: Archive Photos 842, 846, 849
Image Select: 769, 770, 800, 802, 805, 809b, 826a
Mary Evans Picture Library: 799, 801b, 808, 810b, 816, 822-823
© Munch Museum/Munch-Ellingsen Group/DACS, 1999. Photo: © Munch Museum (Svein Andersen/Sidsel de Jong), 1999 850a
Peter Newark's Pictures: 739a, 743, 746, 751b, 752, 753a, 754b, 759a, 774, 817, 819, 822, 824b, 825, 827, 828, 829, 830b, 831, 832, 833a, 836, 838, 839; © Banco de Mexico/Museos Diego Rivera y Frida Kahlo/Instituto Nacional de Bellas Artes y Literatura 744a
Robert Hunt Library: 731a, 826b
South American Pictures: 765a, 756b, 762, 765b; Chris Sharp 760a; Hilary Bradt 754a; Kimball Morrison 759b; Pedro Martinez 737; Tony Morrison 738, 741b, 742, 747, 748, 751a, 756a, 757, 763, 741a, 760b, 766
Werner Forman Archive: 781

Index

Page numbers in *italic type* refer to illustrations and captions.

Page numbers in *italic type* refer to illustrations and captions.

Page numbers in *italic type* refer to illustrations and captions.

864

Page numbers in *italic type* refer to illustrations and captions.